The
Green Bag Travellers

Books by Anthony Burton

Non-Fiction

THE CANAL BUILDERS
CANALS IN COLOUR
REMAINS OF A REVOLUTION
CANAL
THE MINERS
JOSIAH WEDGWOOD
BACK DOOR BRITAIN

Fiction

THE RELUCTANT MUSKETEER
THE MASTER IDOL
THE NAVIGATORS
A PLACE TO STAND

Humour

A PROGRAMMED GUIDE TO OFFICE WARFARE
THE JONES REPORT

The

Green Bag Travellers

Britain's First Tourists

===

ANTHONY and PIP BURTON

ANDRE DEUTSCH

First published 1978 by
André Deutsch Limited
105 Great Russell Street London WC1

Printed in Great Britain by
Ebenezer Baylis & Son Limited
The Trinity Press, Worcester, and London

British Library Cataloguing in Publication Data

Burton, Anthony
  The green bag travellers.
  1. Tourist trade – Great Britain – History
  I. Title   II. Burton, Pip
  338.4′7′9141   G155.G7

  ISBN 0 233 96761 3

'The carriage of baggage may justly be considered an inconvenience; it is therefore proper to take as few things as possible; these carried in a light green bag (I would on no account recommend a blue one, as that might occasion you to be mistaken for a lawyer).'

Daniel Carless Webb, *Four Excursions Made to Various Parts of Great Britain*, 1812

Contents

List of Illustrations	*page*	9
1	Introducing the Travellers	11
2	Chasms and Crags	32
3	Tourist Attractions	54
4	A Changing World	75
5	The Rich Man in his Castle, the Poor Man at his Gate	102
6	Travellers in a Foreign Land	122
7	End of an Age	141
	Bibliography	145
	Index	149

Illustrations

===

TRAVELLERS AND TRAVELLING
(*between pages 20 and 21*)

Title-page of 'A Tour in Scotland'
Portrait of William Mavor (*Dr Robb-Smith, Woodstock*)
'Doctor Syntax and Bookseller' by Rowlandson
View near Hagley, Worcester
A stage-coach near Launceston
A 'Picturesque Road Map' of 1802, the London to
Worcester road

THE PICTURESQUE
(*between pages 52 and 53*)

An idealised picturesque landscape by William Gilpin
Portrait of William Gilpin by H. Walton
(*National Portrait Gallery*)
Gordale Scar
The Devil's Bridge, Cardigan
Snowdon and Llanberis Lake
A bridge near Scarborough
Fingal's Cave as seen by Faujas St-Fond
St-Fond with a blacksmith's family

TOURIST ATTRACTIONS
(*between pages 84 and 85*)

Alnwick Castle, Northumberland
Willersley Castle
Two picturesque fragments from a traveller's sketchbook

9

Illustrations

Mixed bathing in Bath
The Crescent, Bath
Shakespeare's birthplace, Stratford-upon-Avon
The beach at Barmouth

INDUSTRY AND THE COMMON MAN
(between pages 116 and 117)

Portrait of Arthur Young by G. Dance, 1794
(National Portrait Gallery)
Sketch of the Bridgewater Canal by Arthur Young
Parys Mountain, Anglesey
The Darby ironworks, Coalbrookdale
Josiah Wedgwood's Etruria works
(Josiah Wedgwood & Sons Ltd)
A forge near Dolgellau
A Welsh landlady, by Rowlandson
A kitchen in Newcastle, by Rowlandson

*Unless otherwise credited all pictures are taken from the
Bodleian Library, Oxford*

1

Introducing the Travellers

===

TRAVEL BOOKS, travel books, travel books! By the end
of the eighteenth century, they fairly deluged from the
presses, topping the best-seller lists of Georgian Britain.
They described a strange land with strange customs, a
country blessed with beautiful and previously undis-
covered scenic marvels. That country was Britain. For this
was the first great age of popular travel, when one's own
country was still a mysterious, unknown land. No wonder
then that the intrepid Londoner, who ventured into the
wilds of Derbyshire, set off on his journey filled with the
excitement of one about to explore the upper Amazon.
Little wonder, too, that on his return he was eager to tell
the world of his discoveries – and the world, it seems, was
equally eager to listen.

In this book, we have tried to recreate the world of the
travellers during a period from roughly the middle of the
eighteenth century to the beginning of the railway age in
the 1830s. We hope to convey the freshness, the excitement of discovery which marked this time when the
British first began exploring their own country for the
sheer pleasure of it. We live in an age when travel seems
to have lost much of its zest. Consider modern air travel.
Encapsulated in a metal cylinder, fed plastic food on plastic
plates, regaled with music designed not to please but to
avoid giving offence, the seasoned jet traveller is whisked
from an air-conditioned hotel in, say, New York to an
identically anonymous, internationally styled building in
Timbuktu. He is exchanging luxuries, and for all the
difference between the two he might as well have stayed

11

at home. The Georgian traveller moved slowly through
the land. He may have travelled shorter distances, but he
had time to look about to satisfy his curiosity on every
aspect of the life around him. By looking at his world, we
can see an approach to travel that is very different from
our own.

In order to recreate the world of the Georgian travellers,
we have drawn heavily on their books, quoting liberally
from those writers who seem to catch the essence of the
time. So, before going any further, it will be just as well to
establish a few facts about these books and, more especially, about their authors. Take two examples, William
Mavor and Thomas Pennant; two very different per-
sonalities but both successful and popular travel writers.

William Mavor (1758–1837) lived at Woodstock, near
Oxford. He was ordained as a clergyman, but devoted his
time to teaching: or, to be more accurate, devoted some of
his time to teaching, for his interests were nothing if not
varied. In his professional life, he was kept busy running
his own school – which he seldom failed to advertise in
his books.

A most delightful and healthy situation
at the
ACADEMY
at
Woodstock, Near Oxford.
Young gentlemen are genteelly boarded, and
expeditiously qualified for the University,
the various Branches of Trade,
or private life.
By the Rev. William Mavor LL.D.
Terms

	£	s
Board and lodging	15	15
Education	4	4
Washing	1	1

At least education cost more than washing. But Mavor
was no ordinary schoolmaster. He taught by his very own

Chrestomatic system of education – using carefully selected passages from various works to teach language and other 'useful' subjects. And this was by no means the end of his educational innovations. He invented a 'universal stenography', a form of shorthand of quite staggering complexity. He also produced educational books of all kinds and varieties, ranging from *The Lady's and Gentleman's Botanical Pocket Book* to *Universal History, Ancient and Modern*. These activities apparently left him plenty of spare time to write poetry, which was also published even though it was, to be honest, not particularly good. Here is the beginning of his 'Ode to Nature'.

Amid the variegated scene
Of blossoms, flowers and herbage green,
Where twining shrubs enamour'd grow,
And oaks adorn the mountain's brow;
Enraptured let me tune the lay,
And sing of Nature, ever gay.

After all that, it's no surprise to discover that when this man took to travelling, he showed an interest in anything and everything that came his way. Such a breadth of interest is one of the great fascinations of the early travel accounts – scenery, people, even the extraordinary rapid growth of industry at that time, all came into focus.

Mavor was a clergyman, a group quite widely represented among these writers, but the largest single group is more difficult to categorise. There is a clue in the Mavor advertisement. It consists of those who were educated for private life. Thomas Pennant was just such a one, and a very busy private life it was too. He was a competent naturalist, an enthusiastic traveller and a prolific writer, as he himself explained in a modest autobiographical note.

ᵗⁱⁿⁿ astonished at the multiplicity of my pub-
ˑˡˡᵧ when I reflect on the various
ᵇ my lot to discharge. As father
'd of a small but very numerous

tenantry, and a not inactive magistrate, I had a great share of health during the literary part of my days, much of this was owing to the riding exercise of my extensive tours, to my manner of living, and to my temperance. I go to rest at ten; and rise winter and summer at seven . . . I avoid the meal of excess, a supper; and my soul rises with vigour to its employs and (I trust) does not disappoint the end of its Creator.

Mr Pennant was clearly a somewhat quirky individual. He was also unusual in choosing to travel on horseback, but his opposition to any other mode of transport was robust. 'I consider the absolute resignation of one's person to the luxury of a carriage, to forebode a very short interval between that, and the vehicle which is to convey us to our last stage.' He was one of the first to travel Britain just for the pleasure and interest of it, and the books in which he described his various tours became immensely popular. They were translated into French and German, but his main impact was on his own countrymen. His obituary in the *Annual Register* of 1804 made the point of mentioning his 1769 tour of Scotland, 'a country at that time as little known to its southern brethren as Kamtschatka. He published an account of his journey which proved that the northern parts of Great Britain might be visited with safety, and even with pleasure.' There were many who followed Pennant, both by repeating his journeys and by setting down their own accounts. They were a motley crew, pursuing a whole range of individual interests, or simply following where natural curiosity led them.

A French writer, Faujas St-Fond, for example, was a professor of geology, so it is not too surprising to find that things scientific occupied his thoughts a good deal. There was a kind of international freemasonry among scientists which gave him an entrée into the laboratories of the famous, with occasionally startling results. On a visit to the anatomist John Sheldon, he was shown the body of young woman who, after death, had been quite literally pickled. He confessed afterwards that he might have taken a somewhat different view of Sheldon's detached commentary on the state of preservation of the corpse had he known at the time that the body in question was that of the doctor's ex-mistress. Fellows of the Royal Society are altogether more respectable these days, and would be inclined to disapprove of their president pickling his mistress: they would be hardly less disapproving of his carving his name in the rocks at a famous beauty spot. Yet St-Fond found the name of the then president, Sir Joseph Banks, carved at the entrance to the Devil's Arse Cavern – a place which was as interesting as and more attractive than its name suggests. The cavern, near Castleton, had a 120-foot wide entrance, and was so roomy inside that it served as a workshop for two manufacturers and housed several families.

Other specialists included the agriculturalist Arthur Young, who travelled in order to build up a picture of the state of farming in the country. But although he and St-Fond were pursuing their own special interests they still found time to look about them and record the habits and pastimes of the people, admire the scenery, take note of the state of the roads and take time off to investigate anything that happened to catch their fancy. Everything was of interest, everything deserved consideration. This universal curiosity led the travellers to spots which would scarcely feature on a modern tourist map. How many of us would spend our holidays visiting new prisons? Yet the Rev. Stebbing Shaw, who declined to say very much about his visit to Oxford on the grounds that quite enough had been written on the subject already, found space to eulogise on the gaol being built next to the castle, ending with the opinion that it would have 'a noble appearance'. This might appear unexceptional were it not that soon after this he was off to Gloucester, to visit the gaol there. Hot in his footsteps came another clergyman, the Rev. Richard Warner, also eager to see Gloucester gaol, while Thomas Pennant wrote a very full account of the gaol at Chester. The latter would clearly seem to have been built more with deterrence in mind than rehabilitation.

Their day confinement is in a little yard, surrounded on all sides by lofty buildings, impervious to the air except from above, and ever unvisited by the purifying rays of the sun. Their nocturnal apartments are in cells seven feet and a half by three and a half, ranged on one side of a subterraneous dungeon in each of which are often lodged three or four persons. The whole is rendered more (wholesomely) horrible by being pitched over three or four times in the year. The scanty air of their straight prison-yard is to travel through three passages to arrive at them: through the window of an adjacent room; through a grate in the floor of the said room into the dungeon; and finally, through the dungeon through a little grate above the door of each of their kennels. In such places as these are the innocent and the guilty permitted to be lodged, till the law decides their fate. I am sure that humane keeper, Mr. Thomas, must feel many a pang at the necessary discharge of his duty. The view I had of it, assisted to raise the idea of a much worse prison, where

No light, but rather darkness visible
Served only to discover sights of woe.

The obvious explanation would be that this was all part of the movement towards prison reform, but most writers simply describe with no hint of criticism. The Rev. Shaw, for one, seems to have had a passion for gaols much as others have a passion for old castles.

Whatever their reasons for travelling, the tourists all had one characteristic in common – they were rich, though not necessarily the very rich. The aristocracy generally favoured the Grand Tour of Europe; Britain could only offer the Less Grand Tour. But they were rich enough for all that. A constant cry of the modern age is 'look at the cost!' followed by a mournfully nostalgic comparison with 'the good old days'. A brief glance at

Georgian travel costs should be enough to dispel that sort of historical dream world. William Kitchiner, a gentleman whose books provide a regular fund of practical information on travellers and travelling, gave some detailed costings for a man and his wife taking a thirty-seven day tour through the northwest of England and North Wales in the 1820s. The 'Chariot' was hired out at two guineas per week, horses six guineas per week, with the coachman coming rather cheaper at 6s 6d per day. That made a total of £59 8s for the actual travelling expenses. On top of that they had to add the cost of food and accommodation at £58 12s, making a grand total of £118. To put that in some sort of perspective, you could compare it to what another traveller described as 'the present exorbitant wages' paid to cotton workers of two shillings a day. In other words, the cost of the tour represented well over three years' wages for the industrial worker. No, travelling was definitely not a poor man's pastime.

'Gentlemen of independent means': that is as good a description as any of the tourists, and within that broad category could be found a fair sprinkling of visitors from other European countries. For the latter, costs could well be even higher than for the native travellers, as they were often afflicted by that universal scourge, which has yet to be cured – the overcharging of foreigners. Faujas St-Fond had this to say after being badly stung at the Bull's Head in Manchester. 'The best thing that poor strangers can do in such a case is to pay the money. Travellers are equally likely to this sort of extraction in Italy, Germany and France, as in England; but in neither is it general or derived from national character. It must be imported to a few individuals only, who have lost all feelings of delicacy and justice, but who make a very wrong calculation with respect to their real interests, as they soon destroy both their own reputation and that of the houses they keep.' It is refreshing to find that though the travel writers were inclined to call a spade a 'manually manipulated agricultural implement', they were ready to call the Bull's Head the Bull's Head.

The travellers had not only to be rich, but also to have a good deal of spare time on their hands. The invaluable Dr Kitchiner provides the information that six to seven miles an hour was reckoned a pretty good speed for carriage horses, so a sizeable tour could scarcely take less than a month and often a deal longer. But then there were many in Britain who were rich enough and had time enough for touring, just as there had been for centuries. And that brings us right to a very basic question. Why did tourism not become popular until about the middle of the eighteenth century? The simplest answer is that it was only then that anyone could be expected to gain real pleasure from travelling. Roads before that time were foul, clinging morasses over which the wayfarer fought for the firm ground against all the other road users: herdsmen with their cattle, goose girls with their flocks; great heavy, lumbering carts that sank almost to their axles in the mud. Today we can hardly appreciate just how bad they really were. After reading an account of a traveller falling into a pothole and drowning in the middle of the highway, it is not difficult to understand why ladies and gentlemen might prefer the comforts of home. The eighteenth century was the great age of road building – the age of the turnpikes, the Georgian equivalents of the motorways which made it possible for the carriages to achieve that splendid seven miles per hour. But what was this new, improved travel service really like? How comfortable and convenient was a tour of Georgian Britain? From many of the descriptions, it appears that in spite of the improvements, the traveller needed to be a pretty hardy individual.

There were a number of options open, a variety of ways of moving around the country. The stage-coach is the method that probably comes first to mind. Years of conditioning by Christmas card manufacturers have firmly fixed the picture in our minds of jolly people waving out of coach windows while postillions blow enthusiastically on startlingly long post-horns. The sun always shines and if – as is often the case, the image makers having

Christmas in mind – there is snow on the ground, then it is a permanently sparkling white. Day's end comes with the arrival at the coaching inn where the landlord, even jollier than the passengers, greets his guests with glasses of steaming hot punch. If, heaven forbid, there should be a trace of danger in the journey, then it came with the 'Stand and deliver' cry of the highwayman. But that gentleman is invariably depicted as just that – a gentleman. He relieved travellers of their purses with a few genteel words, and his kissing of the ladies' hands sent such a flutter through the bosoms of matrons and maidens that the loss of an emerald ring was a small price to pay for such a thrilling encounter. Alas, reality was considerably drabber than fiction.

Our card manufacturers showing the stage setting off on its journey give a somewhat misleading impression, for stages frequently left at distinctly anti-social hours. The Edinburgh stage, for example, used to leave the Rose and Crown in St John Street, London at 4 a.m., an hour when even the most conscientiously jolly of landlords might be forgiven a certain sleepy sullenness. And once under way, the passengers might also have been hard put to retain their good humour. Comfort was not all that it might have been, especially for those who were unfortunate enough to miss the inside seats and had to travel on top. Travellers taking Dr Kitchiner's no doubt sound advice must have looked less like cheery human beings and more like over-stuffed scarecrows. 'If circumstances compel you to ride on the outside of a Coach, put on Two Shirts and Two Pairs of Stockings, turn up the collar of your Great Coat and tie an handkerchief round it, and have plenty of dry Straw to set your feet on.'

Sound advice: two travellers on the London to Bath stage in the winter of 1812 were found, when the coach arrived at Chippenham, to have frozen to death. The cold, however, was only one of the hazards, as the German tourist Charles P. Moritz discovered when he travelled on the outside of the stage from Leicester to Northampton.

The getting up alone was at the risk of one's life; and

when I was up, I was obliged to sit just at the corner of the coach, with nothing to hold by but a sort of little handle fastened on the side. I sat nearest the wheel, and the moment that we set off, I fancied that I saw certain death await me. All I could do, was to take still faster hold of the handle, and to be more and more careful to preserve my balance.

The machine now rolled along with prodigious rapidity over the stones through the town, and every moment we seemed to fly into the air; so that it was almost a miracle that we still stuck to the coach, and did not fall. We seemed to be thus on the wing, and to fly, as often as we passed through a village or went down a hill.

At last, the being continually in fear of my life became insupportable, and as we were going up a hill, and consequently proceeding rather slower than usual, I crept from the top of the coach, and got snug into the basket . . . As long as we went up hill, it was easy and pleasant. And, having had little or no sleep the night before, I was almost asleep among the trunks and the passages; but how was the case altered when we came to go down hill; then all the trunks and parcels began, as it were, to dance around me, and every thing in the basket seemed to be alive; and I every moment received from them such violent blows, that I thought my last hour was come . . . I was obliged to suffer this torture nearly an hour, till we came to another hill, when quite shaken to pieces and sadly bruised, I again crept to the top of the coach, and took possession of my former seat.

Travellers inside the coach had their own problems of overcrowding. Dr Kitchiner had decided views on stuffiness and his own effective, if drastic, remedy: 'You may let your stick or your Umbrella fall (accidentally) against one of the Windows, i.e. if you are of opinion that it is more advisable to give a Glazier 3s. to replace a pane of Glass, than it is to pay double that sum for Physic to

A

TOUR

IN

SCOTLAND,

AND

VOYAGE TO THE HEBRIDES;

MDCCLXXII .

CHESTER,
Printed by John Monk,
MDCCLXXIV.

Title-page from one of the many anonymous travel
books of the eighteenth century.

The enthusiastic traveller and collector of travel writings, William Mavor.

'A tour indeed! – I've had enough
Of Tours, and such-like flimsy stuff.'
By the end of the Georgian age, booksellers were
inundated by travel books, as the unfortunate
Dr Syntax is here discovering.

The roads the travellers used were rough, the inns
often rougher – a view near Hagley, Worcester.

A crowded stage-coach getting ready to leave
Launceston.

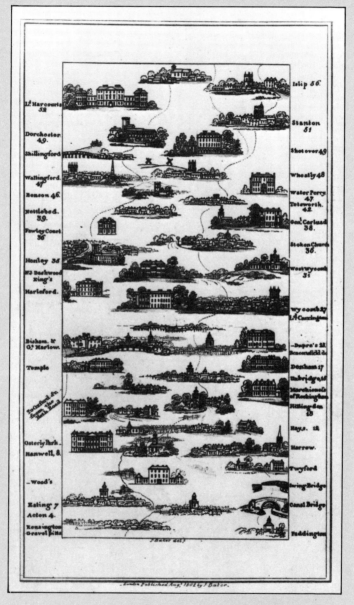

A 'Picturesque Road Map' of 1802, which gave the
traveller his route and showed him what he could see
along the way. This is the London to Worcester road.

remove a Pain in your Head, which you will otherwise get by breathing Foul Air.'

The travellers who suffered nothing worse than bad air could consider themselves lucky. This laconic note in *Felix Farley's Bristol Journal* in August 1783 appeared with no editorial comment and no hint of surprise: 'On Sunday night between eleven and twelve o'clock, as the Salisbury stage was returning to London, it was overturned into a ditch near Basingstoke, owing to the coachman's being very much in liquor.' Clearly all that Christmas card punch was not intended just for the passengers.

Coaches were cramped and confined, and once inside them there was no escape. One's sympathies go out to William Hutton, stuck for hours in the coach for Scarborough in 1803: 'Our bill of lading, besides myself, consisted of a lady with her infant, to which she expected every person should pay the same attention she did: forgetting that although infants are the most engaging of all living things, yet love will not grow with the rapidity of a mushroom. The whole company must submit to the humours of this child, which indicated she did not understand the art of nursing. I allow, a child and a puppy dog may be useful in company; they fill up the gaps in conversation nay sometimes engross the whole.'

An alternative to the stage-coach was the post-chaise, a smaller carriage which also moved from stage to stage – its relation to the coach was rather that of a long-distance taxi-cab to a public bus. A small carriage was the most popular form of transport: the rich drove their own carriages, the less rich hired. Some way behind them in the travellers' social scale were those who went on horseback and, coming a very bad last, the pedestrians. Walking was all very well as an exercise 'for those who are, by the condition in which they are born, exempted from work' but there were warning words from one gentlemanly walker, a Mr Shepherd, who had gone tramping in Wales.

We performed our Tour on foot, but I do not mean to

recommend that mode of travelling; far from it, the inconveniences and difficulties attending a Pedestrian Excursion are many and great. At one time the Roads are rendered so muddy by the Rain that it is almost impossible to proceed; and when, perhaps, you have dragged on at the rate of a mile an hour, you are frequently unable to obtain any accommodation, at least not such as a traveller who has been accustomed to a comfortable Home would be contented with; consequently, you are reduced to the sad extremity of either sleeping in a filthy Bed, or of proceeding to the next place, however wearied. At other times, you are exposed to the inclemency of the Weather, and by wasting time under the shelter of a Tree, or a hedge, are benighted in your Journey, and again reduced to an uncomfortable dilemma. But even allowing you arrive safely and seasonably at the place of destination, you are not then certain of being accommodated, for Innkeepers frequently hesitate to admit those who travel on foot; and in consequence of this, it was sometimes not without the utmost difficulty that we procured a reception.

Charles Moritz also carried out much of his British tour on foot; understandably, given his alarming experiences on the stage-coach. But he found that his appearance on foot produced some strange reactions, and in Burton-on-Trent, the locals actually turned out to hiss him as he walked through the streets. Yet another traveller, commenting on Moritz, concluded that 'a traveller on foot in England is considered as a sort of wild man, or an out-of-the-way being who is stared at, pitied, suspected and shunned, by everybody that meets him.' (Travel writing soon became quite an incestuous business with travellers borrowing from each other's writings, and commenting on each other. It even reached the stage where the houses of the better known tourists, such as Thomas Pennant, became tourist attractions themselves.) The final insult to the enthusiastic pedestrian was delivered to the Rev.

Richard Warner: he was stopped on his walk by two very
ragged local women who, eyeing his best walking outfit,
commented bluntly, 'A luks a grut deal more lik a beggar
than a does lik a gentleman.'

On foot, on horseback, in a carriage, however he made
his way, the traveller could give thanks for the benefit of
the new road system. Benefit? Well, not always. Here is
Arthur Young on the Wigan turnpike in the 1760s – a
description that has often been quoted over the years, but
which bears repeating as a reminder of just how appalling
even a brand new road can be.

> I know not, in the whole range of language, terms
> sufficiently expressive to describe this infernal road.
> . . . Let me most seriously caution all travellers, who
> may accidentally purpose to travel this terrible
> country, to avoid it as they would the devil; for a
> thousand to one but they break their necks or their
> limbs by overthrows or breaking downs. They will
> here meet with rutts which I actually measured four
> feet deep, and floating with mud only from a wet
> summer; what therefore must it be after a winter?

The roads may have been, in general, better than they
had been a century before, but descriptions such as Young's
were not all that rare. The new turnpikes formed a complex web, controlled by an equally complex administrative
system. The roads were privately built, and each Trust
was responsible for maintenance. Some Trusts were
conscientious repairers of their roadway, others merely
conscientious collectors of tolls. Road repairs might consist of no more than shovelling fresh gravel onto the thick
mud in the vain hope that it would not all sink without
trace, and such roads remained horrors well into the
nineteenth century. The traveller might well have been
tempted to take to the water as a relief from all that mud.
The Duke of Rutland visited an island in Tenby Bay in
1797.

We were a good deal tossed about today, so much

indeed that we were frequently near losing our seats. When we were in the bosom of the waves, we were not able to see anything about us, except the white foam of the sea breaking above us. Sometimes we shipped some water, which came in over the gunwale. One of the seamen was obliged to hold the main sheet by a rope, in order that he might be able to let it go immediately in case of a sudden squall. We had two reefs in the sail, but notwithstanding, we were all completely wet to the skin by the spray of the sea, which sometimes rolled into the boat, in thick bodies of water.

He added with true British phlegm: 'Nevertheless we had a good sail.' From the perils of the deep, back to the perils of the highway and some dangerous fellow travellers: dogs, for example. One does not think of dogs as a major hazard to the modern traveller, but they came high on Dr Kitchiner's list of dangers. He gives an alarming account of the results of a bite from a rabid dog: 'There is no real remedy but cutting the part out immediately. If the bite be near a large Blood vessel, that cannot always be done, nor when done, however well done, will it always prevent the miserable victim from dying the most dreadful of deaths!!!' He recommended suitable protection: 'A powerful weapon, and a very smart and light-looking thing, is *an Iron Stick* of about four tenths of an inch in diameter, with a Hook near the Hand, and terminating at the other end in a spike about five inches in length, which is covered by a Ferrule, the whole painted the colour of a common walking Stick; it has a light natty appearance, while it is in fact a most formidable instrument.' Indeed it was, and no doubt was equally effective against robbers and thieves. However, for protection against the latter, Kitchiner considered it rather more practical to have a brace of blunderbusses, which the traveller was to stick prominently out from each of the side windows of his carriage. To complete the traveller's armoury, he recommended double-barrelled pistols with spring bayonets. If such a barrage of weapons was really necessary, then one would think that it was with feelings of immense relief that the traveller reached journey's end. But even inside the inn he was not free from risk, and he was strongly urged to take his own pocket-door-bolts for the bedroom door. Door bolted, pistol and bayonet at hand, the tired tourist could at last relax for a peaceful night.

All this, of course, was taking precautions to extremes, and the vast majority of tourists went undisturbed about their business. Nevertheless, even if they did not go armed to the teeth, if they followed Kitchiner's advice, they trod the land heavily laden. Here is an abridged version of his list of necessities, complete with adverts for his own products.

A portable Case of Instruments for Drawing
A Sketch and a Note-Book
Paper, Ink, – and Pins, Needles, and Thread
A Ruby or Rhodium Pen
Pencils
A folding one Foot Rule
A Hunting Watch with Seconds
A Mariner's Compass
A Thermometer
A Barometer for measuring heights
A One Foot Achromatic Telescope
Dr Kitchiner's Invisible Opera Glass or Traveller's Vade Mecum
A Night Lamp
A Tinder Box
A Traveller's knife
Galoshes
For the Table, Your own Knife and Fork and Spoon will be no small comfort
A Welch Wig is a cheap and comfortable Travelling Cap

He ends the list with a fair comment on the British weather: 'No matter what the Weather or the Season, never go a journey without an Umbrella (the stick of which may contain a Telescope or a Sword) and a Great Coat.' This was followed by a medical list which included such drugs as Dr Kitchiner's Peristaltic Persuaders, alarming sounding laxatives made from pulverised rhubarb, and even more alarming items: 'A *lancet* is indeed necessary for a traveller, because a Lancet which has been used in bleeding a person afflicted with an Infectious Disease may inoculate any other who may be bled with it a short time afterwards.' Having got these few small items together with all the necessary clothing, not forgetting to include a leather sheet to be used on damp beds, the traveller had then only to pack it all away in boxes, cases and trunks.

As time went on, and travel became more popular, with each new traveller rushing his account into print, so the volume of information for the would-be tourist multiplied. Arthur Young provided something in the nature of a Michelin guide to Georgian Britain, jotting down brisk notes on the inns of the country:

> Rotherham. Crown. Very disagreeable and dirty, but very cheap. Hashed venison, potted mackerel, cold ham, tarts, cheese, and a melon, at 1s a head.
> Castle Howard. New Inn. Crowe. An excellent house, but dear and a saucy landlady.
> Manchester. Bull's Head. Mr Bidworth is a most sensible intelligent person, and gives travellers the best information relative to the Duke of Bridgewater's navigation.

E. D. Clarke also came across some troublesome landlords on his travels. He had planned to take a boat from Cardigan to Aberystwyth but the local innkeeper, who made a profit from hiring horses, so intimidated the sailors that Clarke had no option but to take to the saddle. The Welsh, in fact, came in for some fairly severe criticism in a number of quarters. Henry Penruddocke Wyndham issued this warning: 'It may be necessary to apprize the English traveller (lest from the appearance of the inn at Caerphyli he might be discouraged from prosecuting his journey) that he will rarely meet, in his whole tour, with such indifferent accommodations as are to be found at Caerphyli. It requires something more than common curiosity, to excite a stranger to submit to the inconveniences both of bad eating and lodging.'

Today, Caerphilly is famous for its castle and its cheese. Might the latter, at least, provide some compensation for the discomfort? Not according to Mr Wyndham.

The very common cheese of the country sold for two-pence to three-pence a pound: this last article, indeed, was so wretched a nature that few Englishmen would venture to put a second morsel into their mouths. It is made from the combined milk of goats, sheep, mares and cows, and if any cheese should remain from last year's stock, which is often the case, it is then chopped into minute pieces, and remixed with the new. It may easily be conceived that the cheese, by these means, contracts such a hardness, as to be almost proof against the edge of a knife, and such a rankness, that train oil is sweet in the comparison.

There were those, however, such as W. Hutchinson, who were as ready with praise of the inns as others were with blame. He described the landlord of the White Swan at Penrith as 'a man above his rank in sentiments, above his fellows in propriety of manners, his house commodious and clean, his provisions excellent and his attendance prompt and not impertinant.' And Prince Pückler-Muskau, who made two visits to Britain from his home in Germany, extended his commendation to British inns in general. 'In the country, even in small villages, you find them equally neat and well attended. Cleanliness, great convenience, and even elegance, are always combined in them.' And to emphasise the point he quoted the fare supplied by way of breakfast, when all he had asked for was a pot of tea.

In the middle of the table smoked a large tea-urn,

prettily surrounded by silver tea-canisters, a slop basin, and a milk-jug. There were three small Wedgwood plates, with as many knives and forks, and two cups of beautiful porcelain: by them stood an inviting plate of boiled eggs, another 'ditto' of broiled 'oreilles de cochon à la Sainte Menehould'; a plate of muffins, kept warm by a hot water-plate; another with cold ham; flaky white bread, dry and buttered toast, the best fresh butter in an elegant glass vessel; convenient receptacles for salt and pepper, English mustard and 'moutarde de maille'; lastly, a silver tea-caddy, with very good green and black tea.

The total cost was two shillings.

Some travellers took a rather different view, and complained about a lack of hospitality. They might well have been demanding rather more than it was reasonable to expect. The same German prince who was loud in praise of British inns was, not unreasonably perhaps, equally loud in his condemnation of the British climate which, 'if favourable to vegetation, is dreadful for men'. Unreason enters with this anecdote of hospitality not requested but taken.

This morning, at nine o'clock, I rode out on a hired horse, in beautiful weather and a cloudless sky, and before I had been out an hour the most soaking rain wetted me through and through. At last I reached a village, where, in despair at not finding even a gateway under which to take shelter, I sprang from my horse, and seeing a cottage door open, went in, and found two old women cooking something over a fire. In England, everything domestic is held so sacred and inviolable, that a man who enters a room without having cautiously announced himself and begged pardon, instantly excites alarm and displeasure. Although the cause of my intrusion ran in pretty obvious streams from my hat and clothes, I was not very cordially received by the old ladies. But what was the rage and horror of my hostesses 'malgré elles' when my steed, whose sagacity would have done honour to Nestor himself, walked in at the door, and before anything could be done to stop him, took his station in the most quiet and decorous manner before the chimney-piece, and with a look of sly, affected stupidity, began to dry his dripping ears at the fire. I thought the women would have died of rage, and I of laughing. I had such compassion for my poor comrade in misfortune, that I did not like to turn him out by force; and so, – they scolding and storming, I trying to appease them with gentle words, and the more approved eloquence of other silver sounds, – we staid, half by force, half by entreaty, till the storm was a little over, and we were a little dried.

The travellers passed on all kinds of useful tit-bits of information to their fellows – and other morsels of less obvious relevance. While advice on inns was clearly useful, it is difficult to understand the reasoning of George Beaumont and Captain Disney, who added a treatise on coal-mining to their otherwise quite conventional tour. But it could well have been that they realised the treatise would have some practical value, even for the ordinary traveller – for Mrs Morgan, when she visited Wales, found some areas to be pitted with abandoned and unguarded coal shafts. If she had read the mining essay, at least she would have known what to expect.

It is perhaps something of a calumny to describe Mrs Morgan as an 'ordinary' traveller. She provides a splendid and extraordinary female incursion into what often seems a purely masculine activity. Indeed she herself wrote a spirited condemnation of anyone who denied her rights to enter the lists as authoress. 'To those who think a woman cannot find leisure to write, without neglecting either her person or some part of her family duty, I say nothing. They must believe that the sex is formed merely to dress and be admired or for domestic drudgery. Those notions have long ago been exploded by people of polite manners and liberal education.' The firm voice of Women's Liberation was clearly to be heard in Georgian Britain.

After such a catalogue of dangers and difficulties, it might seem surprising that anyone chose to travel at all, let alone for pleasure. But travel they did, and as the eighteenth century gave way to the nineteenth, so crowds of tourists set off on their rounds. A Yorkshireman, Thomas Hurtley, caught the mood of growing enthusiasm for travel when he wrote in 1786: 'An universal rage for Foreign Travel has long occasioned an unaccountable neglect of the Beauties and Wonders of our own Country. Indeed till within these few years a Travelled Englishman either knew not that we had any natural curiosities to admire, or deemed it unfashionable to acknowledge, that there was anything in Britain worth the momentary attention of a man of Taste or ordinary Information. To the honour however of the present times such unnatural prejudices are wearing away apace.'

Each traveller was eager to see the sights described by others, and no less eager to discover new delights, previously unnoticed. They were as interested in the people they met as in the countryside through which they travelled, and from the vast volume of material that came from the presses, there was scarcely a traveller who went without pen and notebook to hand. They were determined to see and record for themselves. Not for them the view commented on by Sir Philip Sidney in the previous century: 'It hath been lately maintained in academical dispute, that the best Travelling is in Maps and good Authors, because thereby a man may take a view of the state of the manners of the World without mixing with the corruption of it.' They were prepared to risk a little corruption for the sake of a new experience.

Once fairly begun, travelling became quite the thing among the gentry. Indeed, by the time the French traveller, Pichot, visited Britain in 1825, it seems to have become a compulsory item in London's social calendar. 'It is time to quit London; it is indeed so unfashionable to stay here, that persons *comme il faut*, who have neither country-house nor post chaise to convey them on a tour of the Lakes, shut themselves up in their apartments, and order their servants to say that they have quitted town.'

Perhaps the most convincing evidence that an activity has achieved genuine popular appeal comes when that activity is satirised – and travellers and travel books easily pass the test. They were fair game for the humorists of the age. One of the best of the satires was Combe's *The Tour of Doctor Syntax*, written in 1812. Syntax made his tour and returned eager to dash into print, only to receive this daunting reply from his publisher.

> *A Tour, indeed! – I've had enough*
> *Of Tours, and such-like flimsy stuff.*
> *What a fool's errand you have made*
> *(I speak the language of the trade),*
> *To travel all the country o'er,*
> *And write what has been writ before.*

Poor Dr Syntax – he was simply too late. The tour books were in full spate. The travellers were on their way.

2

Chasms and Crags

===

But the danger was past – they had landed at last,
With their boxes, portmanteaus, and bags:
Yet at first sight the crew were not pleased with the view,
Which consisted of chasms and crags.

LEWIS CARROLL'S fearless snark hunters might have
been dismayed by such sights, but they were meat and
drink to the British tourists, dashing about the Lake
District or Wales in search of crags, preferably beetling,
and chasms, invariably bottomless. And why not indeed,
for today we are still enthusiastically admiring the same
regions. We accept them as beautiful, we exclaim at their
magnificence. Yet this had not always been the case.
Daniel Defoe, who had toured Britain and produced his
own 'state of the nation' report, had taken no delight in
wild scenery. When he visited Westmorland in the
1720s he took gloomy note that all he could see were
'impassable hills, whose tops, covered with snow, seemed
to tell us all the pleasant part of England was at an end'.
He only began to cheer up again 'when having passed by
Kendal, and descending the frightful mountains, we began
to find the flat country show itself; we soon saw that the
north and north east part of the county was pleasant,
rich, fruitful, and, compared to the other part, populous.'
 Dr Johnson elaborated on a very similar view of
scenery in his description of the Scottish Highlands:

They exhibit very little variety; being almost wholly
covered with dark heath, and even that seems to
be checked in its growth. What is not heath is

nakedness, a little diversified by now and then a stream rushing down the steep. An eye accustomed to flowery pastures and waving harvests is astonished and repelled by this wide extent of hopeless sterility. The appearance is that of matter incapable of form or usefulness, dismissed by nature from her care and disinherited of her favours, left in its original elemental state, or quickened only with one sullen power of useless vegetation.

He then spent some time musing over the possibility of planting trees to cover the rude nakedness of the hills. But already, by the time he made his trip to the Hebrides in 1773, attitudes were beginning to change. Only half a century after Defoe's tour, the frightful mountains were becoming the great tourist attraction of the age: North Wales, the Derbyshire Peaks, the Wye valley, the Scottish Highlands and, most popular of all, the Lake District – these were the new meccas to which the travellers made their pilgrimages.

The discovery of the delights of wild scenery counts as one of those rare events that can be marked down as largely due to the work of one person, in this case William Gilpin. It was Gilpin who first formulated the rules of scenery watching which gave a new measure to natural beauty: was it or was it not picturesque? He is an unlikely candidate for the role of best-selling author and prophet. A clergyman, he began his writing career with a number of weighty tomes on a variety of abstruse theological questions, before turning to travel with his *Observations on the River Wye*, published in 1770. The book was a huge success. It was never out of print for the next fifty years, running to several editions and being translated into the major European languages. It was followed by a succession of other volumes, all titled *Observations on . . .*, followed by the name of the particular region, and ending with the condition 'Relative chiefly to Picturesque Beauty'. All sold well, though none ever matched the popularity of the Wye volume.

The books themselves are rather dull, and indifferently illustrated, and his main dictum sounds unpromising – that a view could be properly labelled picturesque if it had the correct colouring, proportions and lines to look good in a picture. Of course, this begs the question. What does look good in a picture? Gilpin never laid down exact rules, preferring to teach by example. In the world of art, he looked towards France and the poetic and romanticised landscapes of Gaspard Poussin and Claude. He looked for a feeling of balance – a heavy mass there balancing a lighter here. He was advocating a retreat from ordered regularity. As in art, so in nature. Gilpin would have nothing to do with tidy, well ordered fields, neat hedgerows, tall, straight trees. He wanted sharp rocks to form a focus of attention, a hedgerow that straggled to give 'a line of interest', a gnarled oak to give welcome relief from a row of poplars. And he pushed his views in book after book, citing one example after another. Ploughing through them, one gets the feeling that Gilpin won the war of artistic taste not by the brilliance of a sudden attack but by steady attrition.

All this gave a new purpose to travellers. They had a definite object in view – to hunt down the picturesque, and they brought to the task the single-minded enthusiasm that the bellman brought to his snark hunting among the chasms and crags. To the true enthusiast it was an exclusive passion. 'Were it not that our plan is taken to confine ourselves to a description of the picturesque views of nature and the effects they have on the imagination', wrote J. Hassell, 'than in making observations on men and manners, we could mention other anecdotes.'

To get some idea of what inspired such single-minded devotion, one has to turn to the books themselves, especially the Wye tour. Here the rules of the picturesque were clearly stated, and amply illustrated in both words and pictures. Gilpin began by setting out his aims and general principles. 'The following little work proposes a new object of pursuit: that of not barely examining the face of a country: but of examining it by the rules of picturesque beauty: that of not merely describing; but of adapting the description of natural scenery to the principles of artificial landscape; and of opening the sources of those pleasures, which are derived from the comparison.' A good example of the system at work followed with this description of Goodrich Castle.

> After sailing four miles from Ross, we came to Goodrich Castle; where a very grand view presented itself; and we rested on our oars to examine it. A reach of the river forming a noble bay, is spread before the eye. The bank on the right, is steep, and covered with wood; beyond which a bold promontory shoots out, crowned with a castle, rising among the trees. This view, which is one of the grandest on the river, I should not scruple to call *correctly picturesque*; which is seldom the character of a purely natural scene.
>
> Nature is always great in design; but unequal in composition. She is an admirable colourist; and can harmonize her tints with infinite variety, and inimitable beauty; but is seldom so correct in composition, as to produce a harmonious whole. Either the foreground, or the background, is disproportionate: or some awkward line runs across the piece: or a tree is ill-placed; or a bank is formal: or something or other is not exactly what it should be. The case is, the immensity of nature is beyond human comprehension. She works on a *vast scale*; and, no doubt, harmoniously, if her schemes could be comprehended. The artist in the mean time, is confined to a span. He lays down his little rules therefore, which he calls the *principles of picturesque beauty*, merely to adapt such diminutive parts of nature's surfaces to his own eye, as come within its scope.

The essence of Gilpin lies in that one word 'correct' – Nature, alas, did not always manage to get things right on her own, but luckily Mr Gilpin was on hand to suggest the necessary corrections. He was all for improving the scenery, and we rejoin him a little further along his way, quite dismayed by the distant view of Tintern Abbey, but ready to put things right. 'Though the parts are beautiful, the whole is ill-shaped. No ruins of the towers are left, which might give form, and contrast to the wall, and buttresses and other inferior parts. Instead of this, a number of gabel-ends hurt the eye with their regularity; and disgust by the vulgarity of their shape. A mallett judiciously used (but who durst use it?) might be of service in fracturing some of them.' Heaven alone knows what devastation Gilpin might have wreaked on the monuments of Britain, and all in the name of fitting them into a picturesque pattern, had he been granted a free hand. However, closer inspection of the abbey revealed a more satisfactory state of affairs, with ivy covering the walls, moss and lichen on the rubble. Altogether it was 'a very inchanting piece of ruin'. By the time Prince Pückler-Muskau visited the site in the 1820s, the ruins had reached a state of dilapidation to satisfy the most discerning of 'picturesque' travellers.

The ruins have received just that degree of care which is consistent with the full preservation of their character; all unpicturesque rubbish which could obstruct the view is removed, without any attempt at repair or embellishment. A beautiful smooth turf covers the ground, and luxuriant creeping plants grow amid the stones. The fallen ornaments are laid in picturesque confusion, and a perfect avenue of thick ivy stems climb up the pillars and form a roof over-head. The better to secure the ruin, a new gate of antique workmanship, with iron ornaments, is put up. When this is suddenly opened, the effect is most striking and surprising. You suddenly look down the avenue of ivy-clad pillars, and see their grand perspective lines closed, at a distance of three hundred feet, by a magnificent window eighty feet high and thirty broad; through its intricate and beautiful tracery you see a wooded mountain, from whose sides project abrupt masses of rock. Overhead the wind plays in the garlands of ivy, and the clouds pass swiftly across the deep blue sky.

As a result of Gilpin's travels and travelogues, the Wye valley became established as a tourist area, and boat trips down the river to take in the scenery and the ruined castles and abbey between Goodrich and Chepstow became immensely popular. But even at its most popular, the Wye never achieved the 'top of the polls' status of the Lake District. Here was everything the picturesque heart could desire – lake and mountain, ivied cottage and rough stone wall, stream and cascading waterfall, even Druidic circles to add a touch of romance.

If Gilpin discovered the picturesque in general, then the specific discovery of the charm of the Lakes belongs to Dr John Brown. In his description of Keswick all the elements were combined which were to be the marks of the truly picturesque.

Instead of the narrow strip of a valley which is seen at Dovedale, you have at Keswick a vast amphitheatre, in circumference about twenty miles. Instead of a meagre rivulet, a noble living lake adorned with every variety of wooded islands . . . on the opposite shore, you will find rocks and cliffs of stupendous height, hanging over the lake in horrible grandeur, the woods climbing up their steep and shaggy sides, where mortal foot never yet approached; on those dreadful heights the eagles build their nests: a variety of waterfalls are seen pouring from their summits, and tumbling in vast sheets from rock to rock in rude and terrible magnificence: while on all sides of this immense amphitheatre the lofty mountains rise round, piercing the clouds in shapes as spiry and fantastic as the very rocks of Dovedale. To this I must add the frequent and bold projections of the cliff into the lake, forming noble bays and promonteries . . .

Were I to analyse the two places into their
constituent principles, I should tell you that the full
perfection of Keswick consists of three circumstances,
beauty, horror, and immensity united; the second of
which is alone found at Dovedale . . . To give you
a complete idea of these three perfections, as they
are joined at Keswick would require the united
powers of Claude, Salvator and Poussin. The first
should throw his delicate sunshine over the cultivated
vales, the scattered cots, the groves, the lake and
wooded islands. The second should dash out the
horror of the rugged cliffs, the steeps, the hanging
woods, and foaming waterfalls; while the grand
pencil of Poussin should colour the whole with the
majesty of impending mountains.

Here are the key words of the picturesque movement –
horrible, dreadful, stupendous, terrible. It is the language
of the Gothick novel: there is the same delight in having
the spine well and truly chilled, but always with the
reassuring knowledge that the danger is remote, the
perils only to be vicariously enjoyed. The travellers in
the lakes enjoyed good roads and could look forward to a
comfortable inn at the end of the day; and from this
secure base they could suffer the refined pleasure of
imagining themselves clinging to the vertical cliffs or
plummeting earthwards from the inevitably giddy heights.
The picturesque writers thrive on hyperbole. Those
unscaleable heights are, in truth, eminently scaleable.
There is scarcely a peak in the area that cannot be reached
with remarkably little exertion. But the travellers wanted
to feel that the peaks were stupendous, the cliffs grand
beyond compare. They were happy to nod in patriotic
agreement when the evangelists of the picturesque told
them that no country in the world was as picturesque
as Britain, with its wild scenes and crumbling Gothic
ruins. It really did not matter if the enthusiasts who
put this point of view had never travelled abroad to
see the Alps or the Pyrenees – the traveller in Britain

was quite content to be told he was getting the best.

Even without sitting down to a formal study of the rules of picturesque landscape, the elements soon became recognisable. The scenery had to be wild and irregular and if any works of man appeared at all, then they had to be ruined and half-way back to nature. An oak tree in a field was of little interest to the picturesque tourist unless it was twisted, gnarled, ivied or, best of all, struck by lightning. A placid river was nothing as compared to a tumbling mountain stream, a gentle slope less interesting than a jagged cliff. But although the ingredients could all be described in detail, it was also essential that they should be mixed in the right proportions. So the scenic experts drew up careful instructions for the uninitiated. Gilpin broke into verse which was – no pun intended – as pedestrian as his prose.

> *Next survey*
> *The distant lake; so seen, a shining spot:*
> *But when approaching nearer, how it flings*
> *Its sweeping curves around the shooting cliffs.*
> *Mark every shade its Proteus-shape assumes*
> *From motion and from rest; and how the forms*
> *Of tufted woods, and beetling rocks, and towers*
> *Of ruined castles, from the smooth expanse,*
> *Shade answering shade, inverted meet the eye.*

Here is the germ of the work of the Lake poets. What Gilpin began, Wordsworth and the rest were to continue, and in rather better style. There were other writers who felt that such general instructions on the viewing of scenery were nowhere near exact enough as a guide for the average traveller. Worried that a tourist might visit a lake or hill and not notice the view – or, worse still, admire the wrong view – they gave detailed notes on 'stations', spots to stand so that everything was seen just as it should be. And they were nothing if not exact in their directions. You are visiting Coniston? Then here are the instructions from West's *Guide to the Lakes* to send you on your way to Station 3. 'After crossing the common, where grows a picturesque yew tree on the right hand, and a small peninsula rushes into the lake on the left, crowned with a single tree, enter the grove and pass a gate and bridge that crosses a small rivulet. Look for a fragment of dark coloured rock on the margin of the water, and near it will be found the best stand for the artist to take the finest view of the lake.' How many ardent seekers after the picturesque trekked across that river to find that particular rock and then jostled for a place to set up their easels or perch with their sketch books? How many went, in blissful ignorance, to the wrong dark rock and enthused happily over the scene? It is easy to make fun of those eager disciples of a particular kind of beauty, and even then there were plenty of critics, prepared to do so. E. D. Clarke wrote in the 1790s:

> It has appeared to me that the world is weary of that word *picturesque*, it is forced in upon every occasion; nay, one gentleman, the grand master of landscape, has contrived with the aid of a few muddy sketches, to swell that word to a volume. It is for this reason, that I turn neither to the right nor to the left to visit the mouldering fabrics of my fore-fathers, unless something remains to be said of them besides the *picturesque beauty of their situation.*

Jane Austen, ever quick to turn an ironic eye on such human foibles, contrasted the sensibility of Marianne Dashwood with the unromantic sense of Edward Ferrars, and his views on the picturesque.

> 'I like a fine prospect, but not on picturesque principles. I do not like crooked, twisted, blasted trees. I admire them much more if they are tall, straight and flourishing. I do not like ruined, tattered cottages. I am not fond of nettles, or thistles, or heath blossoms. I have more pleasure in a snug farm-house than a watch-tower – and a troop of tidy, happy villagers please me better than the finest banditti in the world.'

Marianne looked with amazement . . .

There were quite a few who shared Edward Ferrars' priorities, judging a landscape less by its rugged splendours and more by the evidence it showed of cultivation or use. The Duke of Rutland toured Wales in 1797 and headed south from Brecon over the wild moors and through the deep valleys of the region. Romantic and wild as the scenery was, it did nothing to gladden the heart of the Duke, who viewed it with deep gloom and pronounced all to be a scene of 'dreariness, desolation, and wildness'. But the melancholy passed. 'We now at last were cheered with the sight of Merthur [sic], and the iron forges (of which there are three about the town) sending forth large volumes of smoke.' However exaggerated we may find some of the descriptions of scenery in the picturesque travel books, they are not as bizarre as this. There can be few tourists today who would be happy to trade mountain and moorland for the smoking iron works of Merthyr Tydfil.

In spite of detractors, in spite of those tourists who insisted on preferring utility to beauty, the apostles of the picturesque continued to make more and more disciples, and soon the cult of the picturesque was absorbed into that wider movement which led towards full-blooded Romanticism. The idea of a scene of ruins covered with ivy, oaks riven by thunderbolts and craggy mountains shattered and worn by the power of wind and rain led almost inevitably to rapturising over the elemental forces themselves and the essential wildness of nature. The sea was added to the lakes as a tourist attraction, and not merely as a place to take a polite dip for the good of one's health, but as a wild force. And with the admiration of a wild sea came the equal fascination with the wild coastline. Mrs Morgan, on her tour to Milford Haven, was enraptured by her first acquaintance with the Pembrokeshire coast.

> I have now, for the first time in my life, seen the
> sea. This assertion startles you, for you know that
> I have very frequently seen it on the Suffolk coast.

But I assure you the Suffolk sea is very different from the Pembrokeshire sea. The former is a dead flat, of a thicky, muddy hue, with no objects to diversify the 'wild horrors of the deep' save a few dirty colliers, or some small craft in their heavy course, and some starved seagulls hovering over it. Nor is the sea at Dover or the white cliffs that overhang it to be compared with this! . . . the sea suddenly broke in upon my sight at St Bride's Bay and presented the grandest assemblage of objects that can meet together in one view. The bay is like an immense bason, filled with crystal water and begirt on every side except where it opens to the main ocean, with rocks, promontories and mountains. The coves and bays that are formed by those projections, give the most charming variety to the scene, and entirely take away the dreariness and horror which the sea on a flat coast naturally inspires.

The ideal was reached when some suitably 'horrible' sight was matched by equally horrible weather. Writer after writer was sent into ecstasies by the sights and sounds of nature at its most fearsome. Thomas Hurtley visited Gordale Scar in the Pennines and his account can stand as an example for many more.

The gloomy melancholy day suited well with the savage aspect of the place; and although my mind, from the frequent adorations I have paid here ought to have been proof against surprise, yet just on turning the corner of the Scar where the fissures hardly are asunder, and seem closing, directly over you – Good Heavens! What was my Astonishment! – The Alps, the Pyrenees, Loch Lomond, or any other Wonder of the Kind at no time, (says an eminent Tourist and Philosopher) exhibit such a Chasm: – but at this instant, a dreadful peal of Thunder, which if I had not been stupid beyond conception I ought to have been prepared for, burst upon me.

Struck with indescribable Terror and Astonishment, the natural apprehensions of instant destruction being over, a man must have been dead to rationality and reflection, whose mind was not elated with immediate gratitude to the Supreme Architect and Preserver of the Universe.

If the writing is inflated, we have to remember that an expedition to Gordale Scar was quite daring: indeed, to go to any of the remote mountain areas was something of an adventure to those ladies and gentlemen who took the first tentative steps, though in fact, of course, the areas were well known to shepherds, herdsmen and the like.

For the great majority of travellers who followed where others led, the excitement was vicarious. Though they exclaimed with awe at the prospect of scaling the mighty mountains, and shuddered at the suggestion of being caught in a storm at sea, they stayed safely in the valleys, and never ventured to sea unless the water was calmed to a gentle ripple. The hills they *did* climb were those with the gentler slopes, such as the Malverns. But if the climb was gentle, the view from the top was as grandly dramatic as that from many a fiercer peak. The Malverns found a worthy champion in the Rev. Stebbing Shaw.

The day being favourable and pleasant, I scarce remember a more enchanting excursion without a possibility of fatigue from so gradual an ascent on nature's carpet, and in little more than half an hour we gained this summit of perfection. . . . We mount the high tops of a Skiddaw, or Ben Lomond, and are lost in wonder and admiration of those immense heaps of rocks that tower around us; they are undoubtedly formed for astonishment and delight and are the source of sublimest ideas; but let not these alone engross our whole attention or alienate our affections entirely from other objects; let us cast our eye a while on this extensive scenery around us and

43

compare the difference; on one side, a champain of
the richest cultivation possible, interspersed with
innumerable mansions, lawns, woods, and the other
golden plantations of the country; peopled with
chearful and thriving towns, and enlivened by the
busy streams of the Severn, and the Avon. These
are the principal features in the Vale of Evesham;
on the opposite side are various winding vallies,
mingled with hop-grounds, gardens, seas and swell-
ing hills of verdant wood, all sweetly softened by the
mellow light of Autumn and enriched by a majestic
range of mountains . . . In short nothing is here
wanting to constitute the beautiful, but here is a
deficiency in those two grand composites of the
north, rock & lakes, to constitute the sublime. With
these additions, we should then find an absolute
perfection.

The Malverns were beautiful but not quite sublime:
Snowdon met all criteria. It had the additional advantage
that although it appeared far more impressive, it was
little more effort to climb than the Malverns. And the
views from the top could be superb. 'How shall I describe
to you the infinitely variegated prospects we enjoyed
from the summit; lakes, mountains, seas, rivers, plains,
woods and islands lay before us, in the greatest diversity.
We saw distinctly the north of England, the greatest part
of Wales, Cheshire, Shropshire, Ireland, the Isle of Man
and Scotland. I doubt whether so extensive a circular
project is to be seen in any part of the terraqueous
globe.' Mr J. Cradock, who was rewarded with this
view, was lucky, not to say imaginative: Thomas Pennant
was one of many who found that the Welsh climate came
between himself and the scenery.

The sky was obscured very soon after I got up. A
vast mist enveloped the whole circuit of the mountain. The prospect down was horrible. It gave an
idea of numbers of abysses, concealed by a thick
smoke, furiously circulating around us. Very often a

gust of wind formed an opening in the clouds, which gave a fine and distinct vista of lake & valley. Sometimes they opened only in one place; at others, in many at once, exhibiting a most strange and perplexing sight of water, fields, rocks, or chasms, in fifty different places. They then closed at once, and left us involved in darkness: in a small space, they would separate again, and fly in wild eddies round the middle of the mountains, and expose, in parts, both tops and bases clear to our view. We descended from this various scene with reluctance.

Even Pennant, enjoying those brief and exotic glimpses, was more fortunate than many others, who quite simply found the top lost in the clouds or, as E. D. Clarke remarked, 'with its night cap on'.

If most were content to look up at or, at best, tackle the very accessible peaks, there were a few hardy souls ready for sterner stuff. Mrs Radcliffe, one of the few authoresses, was as hardy as any and described her adventures with all the panache one would expect from the writer of the famous Gothic novel *The Mysteries of Udolpho*. She took a guided tour on horseback up Skiddaw via a narrow path which 'wound along steep green precipices, the beauty of which prevented what danger there was of being perceived'. Soon there were the familiar pleasures of horrible scenery as they passed the mountain streams 'which hurrying the sight with them into the abyss, act, as it were, in sympathy upon the nerves, and, to save ourselves from following, we recoil from the view with involuntary horror.' Farther up the mountain, they came out onto the ridge – 'dreadfully sublime' – which was enough to silence the whole party. 'Our situation was too critical, or too unusual, to permit the just impressions of such sublimity. The hill rose so closely above the precipice as scarcely to allow for a ledge wide enough for a single horse. We followed the guide in silence, and, till we regained the more open wild, had no leisure for exclamation.'

Visitors from across the Channel, accustomed to the Alps, were often less impressed by the British mountains. Prince Pückler-Muskau noted tartly, if inaccurately, 'I am now returned, dog-tired, from ascending Snowdon, the highest mountain in England, Scotland, and Wales; which indeed is not saying much.' But he was nothing if not adventurous. He set off, late one afternoon, with a shepherd recruited on the spot to act as guide, for an ascent of Tryfan. They must have been an odd pair, the shepherd and the Prince and as the guide spoke only Welsh they were quite unable to communicate with each other except by signs. Half way up they came to a large bog, which they were forced to wade through, but the Prince was rewarded for his wetting by a scene that impressed even that blasé Alpinist. 'Immediately above the bog a completely different sort of ground awaited us; a wall of perpendicular and compact sharp and ragged rocks, over which we scrambled on hands and feet. The sun had already sunk behind a high mountain sideward of us, and reddened the whole scenery around, as well as the wall on which we hung, with a dark and fiery glow – one of the strangest effects of sunlight I ever beheld. It was like a theatrical representation of Hell.'

They scrambled on until they reached the summit itself: 'The mountain region of Wales lay before us in its whole breadth; peak above peak, solitary, silent, and mighty.' On the descent they had to cross a steep scree slope, the dangers of which were dealt with by Pückler-Muskau with a true *Boy's Own Paper* nonchalance. 'It is very true that one false step would cause inevitable destruction; but this is exactly what one takes good care not to set . . . Anybody who can walk, and has a steady head, may perform such exploits without the slightest danger.' The final part of the journey was a moonlit walk to Capel Curig. It had been quite an outing.

Such famous beauty spots as Ryddol Falls and the Devil's Bridge in Merioneth were sketched, painted and described by literally scores of tourists. At least their popularity helped the locals to a little extra cash, even if the visitors did not always find them over eager to earn it. Clarke discovered the guide to the falls to be a woman living in a hovel surrounded by animals and children. When he arrived she was busy peeling turnips, so the obliging Mr Clarke, either out of sympathy or from a desire to get on with his touring, sat himself down and peeled the turnips with her. Vegetables ready, he was taken off to see the sights. He might have been luckier than he knew in getting to see the falls at all. Henry Wyndham noted of his tour in Wales, 'It is remarkable, that we had hitherto never deviated from the true line of our route, when alone; and that we seldom failed of doing so when we employed a guide . . . This was the precise situation of our Harlech attendant: He would not confess his mistakes, 'till he had led us to the very point of a precipice, from which it was impossible to advance a yard farther, without falling from it.'

If the English tourists mistrusted their Welsh guides, the guides, in the early days of tourism, were even more distrustful of their English employers. Clarke had hired a man to take him and his friends from Bala to Llan-rhaidr, and they were all up in their saddles, when the man duly appeared: 'We perceived his countenance change and betray evident marks of the greatest appre-hension: at last he clandestinely slipt away from us. Astonished at this behaviour, we halted, and sent a person to enquire into the reason of it, who reported, that the guide, perceiving our troop to consist of five, was deterred from advancing with us, by the idea of our murdering him on the mountains. Nor could we persuade him, either by ridicule, or argument, to trust himself with us.'

It might seem rather surprising that, given the popu-larity of the Welsh and English mountains, more tourists did not make for the Scottish Highlands. But it was only as recently as the middle of the eighteenth century that the Highlanders had followed their Bonny Prince on the great march southwards that had ended in the bloody defeat of Culloden. A few travellers did make the journey and found scenes as exciting and picturesque as they could wish. Faujas St-Fond, for example, visited the island of Staffa and the famous Fingal's Cave. No doubt, as a Frenchman, he could expect a friendly reception, and, as a geologist, he would put up with a good deal of inconvenience to visit such a fascinating site.

> I soon arrived at the entrance to this wonderful grotto, which an ancient, but fabulous tradition regards as the palace of the father of Ossian . . . There is no other means of going into the cave, but by proceeding with the utmost precaution along a sort of cornice on the right side about fifteen feet above the surface of the water, and formed of a number of erect basaltic columns, on the broken tops of which one must step with considerable dexterity, at the risk of falling into the sea, which extends to the inmost extremity.
>
> Attention is so much the more necessary here, as the ledge upon which the adventurer treads is entirely perpendicular, in some places not above two feet wide at most and consists solely of unequal prisms, very slippery and constantly wet with the foam of the waves and the exudations from above. The light, which comes from the grand entrance only, diminishes gradually as he proceeds inwards, and thus encreases the difficulty of his path.
>
> I ceased not to view, to review and to meditate upon this superb monument of nature, the form of which bears so strong a resemblance to the work of art though the latter can certainly claim no share of it.

His travelling companion, William Thornton, was the Official Artist to the tour, and was given the decidedly awkward task of producing an accurate drawing of the cave while bobbing about in a small boat on the open sea. Meanwhile Faujas St-Fond was equally busy measuring, taking notes and generally fulfilling his own part as official geologist in the dark, foam-splashed interior. But the efforts were all worthwhile. 'I have seen many ancient volcanoes and I have given descriptions of several superb basaltic causeways and delightful caverns in the midst of lavas. But I have never found anything which comes near this, or can bear any comparison with it.'

Faujas St-Fond was one among many tourists who found that in Britain there were whole tracts of country scarcely known except to a few scattered local inhabitants, areas of great natural beauty available for the enjoyment of those who were prepared to go to the trouble of finding them. For such travellers there was not only the ordinary enjoyment of splendid scenery, but there was the extra thrill of discovery and even a possible spicing of danger. Yet it was a steadily diminishing world they moved in: as each traveller made his discovery, he sung its praises, and drew others after him. Exploitation followed in the wake of discovery. It is a familiar pattern – a wild place is discovered, eulogised and quite suddenly it is wild no more. The process continues to this day, so that the seeker after unspoiled country has to travel further and further. It was the good fortune of Gilpin and the early travellers that they were the first to be attracted to such areas: to them went the thrill of discovery.

The hunters after the picturesque, however, did not limit their searches to the wild. T. H. Fielding in his book on the Lakes could point to another pleasure. 'Although nothing can be more beautiful than cultivated nature, yet, in our topographical researches, a uniformity of objects is too frequently the precursor of satiety, until the expansions vary before us, exhibiting the mouldering castle, the dilapidated abbey, or the ample remains of monastic elegance: the mind is then alive to pleasure of a brighter cast, the wisdom – the ingenuity, of former ages, come before our imagination, only to be suppressed with a sigh, while recollection points to the mutability of time.' This is the familiar world of the romantic ruin. It was here that the traveller could sit, compose his picturesque image and, having done so, people it with figures from the past. Here, indeed, was something for everyone. Given a well-ivied ruin any traveller worth his salt could compose a soliloquy – he could mourn the inevitable passing of time and the inexorable process of decay; he could think of jousting knights and the pageantry of the court; or, if those did not suit, he could conjure up the chilling image of a faithless nun bricked up alive in some forgotten cavity in the walls. But even the most imaginative soliloquiser occasionally found his contemplations disturbed by more mundane matters. 'In walking round St Andrew's,' the Duke of Rutland mournfully noted, 'the ruins of former magnificence dispose to melancholy, but the filth and slovenliness of the place provoke disgust. Dung-hills and ash-heaps are laid at every door, while joining with the occasional rubbish of old buildings, and the preparations for new ones, make the streets almost impossible, whether wet or dry.'

There were few who approached the business of inspecting ruins more solemnly than Thomas Pennant, who saw his principal function as the passing on of solid information. In describing Fountains Abbey in Yorkshire he got off to a suitable and promisingly romantic start: 'in approaching the abbey, the view becomes the more awful; when the greatness of the whole is apparent, as well as the elegance of the parts.' But then, when he got down to the detail, the descriptions became noticeably more mundane. 'But the most striking of all the buildings is the cloisters. The form is very uncommon being a vast extent of strait vault, 280 feet long and 42 broad; divided lengthways by nineteen pillars and twenty arches. Each pillar divides into eight ribs at the top, which diverge and intersect with each other on the roof in a most curious manner.' This was no doubt all very accurate, just the sort of good mathematical information the traveller expected to find in his guide book, but it was not at all the sort of thing to stir the heart and quicken the blood. Henry Skrine struck a more romantic note with his description of Alnwick Castle in Northumberland. 'This proud seat of the Percy family presents us lofty towers and embattled fronts with all the magnificence of a Gothic palace, and strongly inspires the idea of the ancient

grandeur attendant on heroes of romance and chivalry.'
Certainly more stirring, but for the full-blown romantic
view one must turn to our German Prince, who suc-
cumbed completely to the atmosphere of Warwick Castle,
'an enchanted palace decked in the most charming garb of
poetry, and surrounded by all the majesty of history, the
sight of which still fills me with delighted astonishment.'
His description is long and wordy, but it completely
captures the full, rich flavour of the picturesque and
romantic vision. The extract begins with the entrance
into the main courtyard.

> Let your fancy conjure up a space about twice as
> large as the interior of the Colosseum at Rome, and
> let it transport you into a forest of romantic luxuri-
> ance. You now overlook the large court, surrounded
> by mossy trees and majestic buildings, which,
> though of every variety of form, combine to create
> one sublime and connected whole, whose lines now
> shooting upwards, now falling off into the blue air,
> with the continually changing beauty of the green
> earth beneath, produce, not symmetry indeed, but
> that *higher harmony*, elsewhere proper to Nature's
> own works alone. The first glance at your feet falls
> on a broad simple carpet of turf, around which a
> softly winding gravel-walk leads to the entrance
> and exit of the gigantic edifice. Looking backwards,
> your eye rests on the two black towers, of which the
> oldest, called Guy's Tower, rears its head aloft in
> solitary threatening majesty, high above all the
> surrounding foliage, and looks as if cast in one mass
> of solid iron; – the other, built by Beauchamp, is
> half hidden by a pine and a chestnut, the noble growth
> of centuries. Broad-leaved ivy and vines climb along
> the walls, here twining around the tower, there
> shooting up to its very summit. On your left lie
> the inhabited part of the castle, and the chapel,
> ornamented with many lofty windows of various
> size and form; while the opposite side of the vast

quadrangle, almost entirely without windows, presents only a mighty mass of embattled stone, broken by a few larches of colossal height, and huge arbutuses which have grown to a surprising size in the shelter they have so long enjoyed. But the sublimest spectacle yet awaits you, when you raise your eyes straight before you. On this fourth side, the ground, which has sunk into a low busy basin forming the court, and with which the buildings also descend for a considerable space, rises again in the form of a steep conical hill, along the side of which climb the rugged walls of the castle. This hill, and the keep which crowns it, are thickly overgrown at the top with underwood, which only creeps round the foot of the towers and walls. Behind it, however, rise gigantic venerable trees, towering above all the rock-like structure. Their bare stems seem to float in upper air; while at the very summit of the building rises a daring bridge, set, as it were, on either side within trees; and as the clouds drift across the blue sky, the broadest and most brilliant masses of light break magically from under the towering arch and the dark coronet of trees.

Figure this to yourself; – behold the whole of this magical scene at one glance; – connect with it all the associations; – think that here nine centuries of haughty power, of triumphant victory and destructive overthrow, of bloody deeds and wild greatness, – perhaps too of gentle love and noble magnanimity, – have left, in part, their visible traces, and where *they* are not, their vague romantic memory; – and then judge with what feelings I could place myself in the situation of the man to whom such recollections are daily suggested by these objects, – recollections which, to him, have all the sanctity of kindred and blood; the man who still inhabits the very dwelling of that first possessor of the fortress of Warwick, that half-fabulous Guy, who lived a thousand years ago, and whose corroded

One of William
Gilpin's idealised
picturesque landscapes,
with all the
appropriate elements
on view: lake, beetling
crags, wide-spreading
trees and ivied ruin.

William Gilpin,
'inventor' of the
picturesque.

Two romantic spots, much favoured by the hunters after the picturesque. *above* Gordale Scar: 'The Alps, the Pyrenees or any other wonder of the kind at no time exhibit such a chasm.' *left* The Devil's Bridge, Cardigan, an illustration from E. D. Clarke's *Tour*.

Early artists tended to exaggerate the wildness of the landscape: *above* Llanberis Lake and Snowdon.

Even the road was treated as a picturesque object by the enthusiastic amateur artist who stopped off by this bridge on the way to Scarborough.

Very few travellers got as far as the Hebrides and the
spectacular Fingal's Cave. The French geologist
Faujas St-Fond and his party exploring by land and
water.

St-Fond was equally interested in the people of the
country. Here he is being entertained by a blacksmith
and his family.

armour, together with a hundred weapons of renowned ancestors, is preserved in the antique hall. Is there a human being so unpoetical as not to feel that the glories of such memorials even to this day, throw a lustre round the feeblest representative of such a race.

3

Tourist Attractions

==

From the pleasures of the rural scene to the delights of urbanity and sophistication, the tourists were prepared to take all in their stride. Ruins had their appeal, but there was a satisfaction too in viewing the great stately homes, such as Blenheim or Woburn, or admiring the architectural splendours of York or Oxford. And how familiar some of those tourist attractions of Georgian Britain sound – Shakespeare's birthplace, a seaside holiday at Scarborough. We are all quite used to the idea of mansions and manors being turned into thriving businesses, but we tend to think of this as being something new. Not a bit of it. True, the Georgian grandee did not sell tickets at the door, but it was an accepted rule of society that if you were the owner of a fine house, your doors should be open to ladies and gentlemen who wished to view your home and treasures. The tourist who came as a private guest had no compunctions about putting his opinion on public record. He would discuss the setting, the architecture – everything down to the furniture and the pictures on the walls. Here, for example, is the agriculturalist Arthur Young, eulogising Wentworth House and its setting: 'At the very entrance to the park, the prospect is delicious: in front you look full upon a noble range of hills, dales, lakes and woods, the house magnificently situated in the centre of the whole. The eye naturally falls into the valley before you, through which the water winds in a noble stile; on the opposite side is a vast sweep of rising slopes, finely scattered with trees, up to the house, which is here seen distinctly, and stands in the point of grandeur from whence it seems to command all the surrounding country.' He then moved in for a closer inspection: 'This portico is lightness and elegance itself; the projection is bold, and when viewed aslant from one side, admits the light through the pillars at the ends, which is a most happy effect, and adds surprizingly to the lightness of the edifice . . .' and so on for many paragraphs. Young, however, could seldom visit a place without commenting on the husbandry of the owner. The Marquis of Rockingham earned a special commendation for his manures, which 'were too curious to be overlooked . . . one compost of which manure mixed with dung I observed was in so complete a state of corruption, that it cuts like butter, and must undoubtedly be the richest manure in the world.' It must be confessed that manure remained something of a minority interest and other tourists were able to overlook it with perfect equanimity. Even Young, on his stately-home visits, found time for other matters, showed a good deal of interest in house interiors and made detailed notes on paintings, such as these jottings from Kiverton.

> *Rubens* The Four parts of the world. The figures are those of Rubens, but the beasts surprizingly fine; the panther equal to anything ever painted and the crocodile admirably done. The groupe vile.
> *Reynolds* The late Duchess of *Leeds*; a most sweet attitude and exquisite eyes.
> *Titian* Figure of a man and a woman. *Danae* and the golden shower; the colours are pretty good, but the drawing appears to be bad.

Young was clearly a man who made up his own mind on questions of artistic merit and was not one to be overwhelmed by a name – how many of today's travel writers would have the temerity to go into print with a bald criticism of Titian's draughtmanship? William Mavor was equally outspoken, and offered this comment on the paintings of Powis Castle, near Welshpool. 'Several of the paintings, however, possess no superior merit, and they are not disposed with much taste. They are either too few in number or the gallery is too large. Three owls by Rubens, the only picture by that great master in the collection, would probably, at a common sale, fetch less than as many Norfolk turkies.'

Alnwick Castle was another high spot in the itinerary of the travelling critics. At the end of the eighteenth century, that ancient building was renovated in the increasingly popular Gothic style, and Young dropped in to see the work and give it his approbation: 'The apartments are all fitted out in the Gothic taste, and ornamental in a very light and elegant stile . . . the architecture of the new buildings is quite in the castle stile and very light and pleasing.' Thomas Pennant, however, took quite a different view. He was ready enough to be impressed by the outside of the buildings, though he complained about the 'rude statues crowded on the battlements'. He even agreed with Young in finding the apartments elegant, but that for him was no virtue. They were 'incompatible' with the nature of a great castle, and he had no higher opinion of the rest of the new works: 'The gardens are equally inconsistent, trim to the highest degree, and more adapted to a villa near London than the antient seat of a great Baron.' Here we have one of the classic conflicts between the picturesque and the comfortable, with Mr Pennant preferring the grand ruin and the Percy family preferring not to spend their days with draughts down the backs of their necks. In fact the work at Alnwick was remarkably well done, and today is an example of one of the few castles which are comfortable yet still retain the atmosphere of earlier and more austere days. The views of Mary Ann Hanway, who stopped off on her way to Scotland seem more in keeping with modern attitudes:

> The castle has been entirely rebuilt but so as to retain its ancient appearance of plainness and strength. The ramparts which surround it, are mounted with cannon: the statues, formidably armed

cap à pée seem to frown protection on the battlements; and the solemn stillness that invades the
traveller, while he surveys the structure, produce
upon the mind a very pleasing effect.

Given the criticism handed out so lavishly by these
uninvited guests, it is remarkable that the stately-home
owners allowed visitors in at all; but let them in they did,
and the tourists came to look upon it as a matter of right
that they should be able to knock on any door and gain
admission. They certainly took a decidedly dim view of
any house owner who said them nay. John Byng, Viscount
Torrington, went to see Wroxton, the house of Lord
Guilford, and to his deep disgust was informed that the
owner had only recently returned home and wished to be
left in peace. 'Very rude this, and unlike an old courtly
earl! Let him either forbid his place entirely; open it
allways; or else fix a day of admission; but, for shame,
don't refuse travellers who may have come 20 miles out
of their way for a sight of his place.'

One can perhaps forgive anyone not wishing to open
their doors to the waspish tongued Mr Byng, who could
repay hospitality with comments such as this on Willersley
Castle, the home of the *parvenu* industrialist, Richard
Arkwright. 'Went to where Sr R.A. is building for himself a grand house in the same castellated stile as one sees
at Clapham, and *really* he has made a *happy* choice of
ground, for by sticking it up on an unsafe bank, he con-
trives to overlook, not see, the beauties of the river, and
the surrounding scenery. It is the house of an overseer
surveying the works, not of a gentleman wishing for
retirement and quiet. But light come, light go, Sir Rd
has honourably made his great fortune; and so let him
still live in a great cotton mill!'

Yet owners remained happy to open their doors to
Byng and the other tourists. Some great houses, such as
Chatsworth or Woburn, had fixed days for public viewing
and had printed catalogues on sale to visitors – documents
so voluminous and so minutely detailed that the visitors

were quite overwhelmed with information. Such elaborate arrangements for the reception of visitors must have been based on an ideal of hospitality, and once begun continued by their own momentum without anybody knowing quite how to stop them. Vanity played a considerable part. The rich have always enjoyed having their homes and possessions placed on permanent record – so they called up painters to put them on canvas, and allowed in tourists to celebrate them in words. Eaglehurst, on the Hampshire coast, was described by Hassell as 'very whimsical, but neat and agreeable to the sight. On the top of it a round tower is erected which was originally intended to have a full view over the southern shores of the Isle of Wight: but unfortunately the director or architect forgot that the ground on which it stands is not of an equal height with the intervening mountains on the island.' He then added the equally uncomplimentary piece of information that the building was known locally as Luttrell's Folly. But one could console oneself with the thought that the next tourist was just as likely to take a different view.

Whatever reason stately-home owners had for opening their doors, the motive of the servants who rushed forward to act as guides was plain enough – money. In some houses, the servants were notorious for the regularity with which they held out their hands. In return, they offered a guided tour, not always conspicuous for its accuracy. There was, for example, the guide who solemnly informed visitors that a painting of Cleopatra was in the house to celebrate her status as Charles II's mistress. At Chatsworth, the visitor had only to step into the garden for eager gardeners to appear as if by magic to turn on the fountains in exchange for an appropriate fee. And Prince Pückler-Muskau sourly remarked of the aviary at Woburn: 'Here the fourth or fifth attendant awaited us, (each of whom expects a fee, so that you cannot see such an establishment under some pounds sterling).' The tourists wanted nothing more than to wander round at leisure; the servants took the not altogether unreasonable view that if the strangers were going to appear uninvited to demand hospitality, they might as well pay for the privilege.

The great houses often had their own special attractions. Woburn offered some bizarre points of interest: 'On pulling down part of the abbey in 1744, a corpse was found with the flesh so firm as to bear cutting with a knife, though it must have been buried at least 200 years.' The Rev. Warner reported in 1802 that 'Longleat formerly possessed the largest and best-stocked aviary in England containing a variety of rare kinds; but of late years it has been neglected, and exhibits at present nothing particularly curious, except a male and female kangaroo, brought from Botany Bay, and presented by their majesties to the Dowager Marchioness of Bath. They are the only animals of the kind in the Kingdom.' Over at Blenheim, they specialised in making up parties who were then whisked through the house at a spanking pace. Mrs Morgan wrote indignantly: 'Through that house, which would take a week to survey, you are dragged in an hour, and, perhaps, as it was my fate, to be obliged to follow a party, whose numerous absurd questions to the person who conducts you prevents even the agreeable ideas you might have in that short stay.' Exotica at Woburn, wild animals at Longleat, parties hurried through Blenheim! *Plus ça change* . . .

The travellers who knocked on the doors of the country houses and then commented on the architectural quality of what they found there, were just as ready to give the world the benefit of their architectural opinions on other great buildings or, indeed, whole towns and cities. The fact that they had not the least qualification for offering such opinions was immaterial – it was a general tenet of belief that simply by being of the gentry, they had automatically inherited education and good taste along with their other possessions. They asserted their views, however strange they may now seem, with the kind of firm authority that only comes from absolute conviction. One can play a guessing game trying to fit descriptions to subjects. Which house 'is certainly a grand pile; but it has little beauty and I should suppose less convenience'? The answer: Longleat as viewed by William Gilpin. And we find the Rev. Warner pronouncing that the effect of Vanbrugh's work was of 'disgusting the eye, both within and without, by its weight and clumsiness. Had Vanbrugh tried his art in castles and pyramids, edifices which were to resist the shocks of military operations and structures that should endure as long as time itself, he probably would have succeeded; but he certainly mistook the path to fame when his taste led him to design domestic mansions in which, instead of massiveness and ponderosity, we only look for lightness and elegance, just proportion and convenience.' So much for the architect of Blenheim.

It's a similar story when we turn from houses to towns. To find Doncaster described by Arthur Young as 'a very pretty, clean well built town' is scarcely less surprising than to find the same author writing of York Minster: 'The entrance strikes the mind with that awe which is the result of the magnificence arising from vastness; but I never met with anything in the proportion of a Gothic cathedral that was either great or pleasing; the loftiness is ever too great for the breadth, insomuch, that one must bend back the head to be able to view the ceiling.' Most travellers, however, seemed to find that the need to bend the neck was a small price to pay for the pleasure of seeing such a building. Henry Skrine wrote: 'Bold indeed must be the pen which attempts to do justice to the beauties of the finest cathedral in England, which rises far above the level of other churches.' York was very much a favoured stopping off place: it combined great antiquity with a number of fascinating buildings and had the added attraction of its great encircling wall. The city did not, however, escape censure. Mr Hutton looked the place over and found it wanting. 'I am now arrived at what is deemed the second city in the kingdom; which, though a place of note, and great antiquity, rather disappointed me. From what I had read and heard, my expectations were raised above par.' He stayed, however, for two or three days, and set out to question the natives. He was quite horrified to find them unable to provide answers to his queries: 'That a man should live seventy years in a place and not know it! Had I been a native I should have written its history; for there is ample food for the pen!' He was equally scathing over the official guide-book: 'The author of the History of York, speaking of the famous Roman Wall erected by Severus, which crosses the island, falls into a small mistake in calling it two hundred and 32 miles long. But such mistakes are rather excusable, because common; we authors tacitly follow each other, without much examination . . . Had he travelled the wall twice, as I did two years ago, he might have found it only 70 miles, as may be seen in my remarks, which I gave to Mr Nichols, Editor of the Gentleman's Magazine.' Yet for all the criticism of York, its inhabitants and historians, he repented in the end and offered this as his final judgement. 'York is a rich mine of antiquity, well adapted to the antiquarian eye. Having penetrated the vein with some success and more pleasure I departed with regret, because I had not time to search deeper. Fortune had never brought me within one hundred miles of the place, and was never likely to bring me again.'

The antiquarian eye was being increasingly turned towards the British scene. It had sadly to be admitted that there was little in Britain that could compare with the splendours being unearthed in southern Europe, where the excavation of such sites as Herculaneum and Pompeii had led to a new and eager interest in the ancient world. The home tour was certainly, in this respect, second best to its grand relation across the Channel. Antiquarianism, however, was not new to Britain when the tourists began to show interest. Earlier in the eighteenth century, William Stukely had proved an enthusiastic advocate of the ancient world and its physical remains. Later travellers were, in turn, encouraged by the general interest in things classical that spread from Europe and which showed itself in the growing popularity of the classical style in art and architecture. Where the later travellers differed from Stukely was in the attitude towards those antiquities that came their way. Stukely was an archaeologist; too many others were mere plunderers. John Byng, for example, was a lover of monumental brasses, but not of the tedious business of taking rubbings. When he spoke of collecting brasses, he meant precisely that, so that we find him at South Kyne complaining bitterly about the hovering presence of a local farmer at just the spot where there was an especially fine collection of brasses, and finally he had to record: 'I look'd around me but dared not plunder.' A sad day for Mr Byng, but others were more fortunate and plundered away quite happily. There was so little apparent concern for the morality of the deed that we even find Sir Joseph Banks, the highly respectable President of the Royal Society, cheerfully lifting a bone out of an accidentally opened tomb in Chester Cathedral. Some of the most famous of British antiquities suffered appallingly from the thoughtless magpie habits of the Georgian tourists. The great Roman pavement at Caerwent was quite ruthlessly pillaged and, given the attitudes of the gentry, the lack of concern shown by those who were paid to protect it seem a little less surprising. Josiah Wedgwood II made these sad notes in his journal for August 1793:

> From Chepstow we went ye next day 7th to Pontypool to attend a navigation meeting & in our way we stopped at Caerwent to see a roman pavement discovered there some time before. The gentlemen in the neighbourhood when this was first discovered subscribed a sum of Money to build a room over it in order to preserve its nature, but to the shame of the owner of the place we found the room stripped of its roof to cover a brewhouse built at ye adjoining farm & the pavement had suffered very much from having its foundations softened by the rain & the pavement then trod upon & loosened by all who came to see it, so that a very few years such usage

will entirely destroy this fine remain of antiquity.
What adds to the crime we must call it of this gent, is
that the roof was not his property having been sub-
scribed & paid for by ye neighbouring gentry. It is
therefore little better than a theft, & a Gothic theft
too.

He went on to detail the damage done to the pavement,
which involved a good deal of it being broken up, and
then decidedly spoiled the high moral tone by noting that
'as there was a number of these pieces loosened by people
walking on the pavement & swept into a corner of the
room we did not scruple bringing some specimens away
with us.'

The Goths fared little better than the Romans: Thomas
Pennant discovered a woeful scene at Holyrood.

The beautiful piece of Gothic architecture, the church,
or chapel of Holy-Rood-Abbey, is now a ruin, the
roof having fell in, by a most scandalous neglect,
notwithstanding money had been granted by Government to preserve it entire. Beneath the ruins lie the
bodies of James II and James I, Henry Darnly and
several persons of rank: and the inscriptions on
several of their tombs are preserved by Maitland. A
gentleman informed me that some years ago he had
seen the remains of the bodies, but in a very decayed
state; the beards remained on some; and that the
bones of Henry Darnly proved their owner, by their
great size, for he was said to be 7 feet high.

Mr Darnly was probably fortunate that there was no
visiting President of the Royal Society around at the time,
and his bones were left to lie where they were buried.

The one ancient ruin that could not be carried away
piecemeal by eager souvenir hunters was Stonehenge.
Hassell's description of this popular site begins promisingly enough with a consideration of that still con-
troversial problem – how were the stones fixed into place?
But then comes this startling statement: 'The last

peculiarity that I remarked in these stones was their durability – their surfaces are almost impenetrable to the utmost effects of the chisel and mallet.' How long Mr Hassell hacked away with hammer and chisel we do not know, but no doubt there were plenty of others eager to have a go. Our own batch of aerosol paint vandals are non-starters compared with their gentlemanly Georgian counterparts.

Eventually enthusiasm for the antique became so great that antiquities were discovered where none existed. So we find Thomas Pennant describing the strange but perfectly natural rock formations of Brimham Crags in Yorkshire as an 'aggregate of Druidical antiquities'. But apart from the spectacular remains of the ancient world, genuine or otherwise, there were many other places that could be placed in the four-star category of tourist attractions.

High on any popularity list, then as now, was Stratford-upon-Avon. Enthusiasm for visiting Shakespeare's birthplace dated back to the Stratford Jubilee of 1769 when, five years too late, his bicentenary was celebrated – by the townspeople and visitors with readings, music and drama, and by the River Avon with a flood that nearly put a stop to all other activities. Here too the vandals were at work, but with a kind of semi-official blessing, eagerly exploiting anything that could be said to have a connection with the town's most famous citizen. Henry Skrine found bardolatory already well under way when he visited Stratford in 1798. 'Everything here seems devoted to perpetuate the memory of the bard; his picture is suspended opposite to that of his great supporter Garrick in the town hall; his tomb also like that of Medina's prophet, attracts a train of pilgrims scarcely inferior in devotion; and the real, or pretended, remains of his mulberry-tree are dispersed with a fervour, almost equal to that which attends the reliques of popery.' The Rev. Warner confirmed that 'many traces of the respect in which the memory of Shakespeare is held by the inhabitants are sprinkled up and down the place in signs and inscriptions.' He also found the less attractive side of the Shakespeare industry. At the birthplace, he was offered a tobacco-stopper said to have been used by Shakespeare, and lumps of wood said to have come off cupboards and chairs belonging to the playwright. The prices were exorbitant, the origins dubious and he wisely went on his way without an 'authentic' souvenir. Other visitors arrived in time to take part in the systematic dismemberment of any articles connected with the great man. E. D. Clarke gave quite a full description of the process.

> Among the number of curiosities which they shew you at Stratford, must be reckoned the house in which Shakespeare was born, and the remains of the mulberry-tree which he planted. The present possessor of the house is a descendant of Shakespeare's – a poor, illiterate peasant. He shews you a chair which formerly belonged to his great ancestor, but which has been so hacked and mangled by the knives of virtuosos that little of its original form remains.

He then listed just a few of the visitors who made off with quite considerable pieces of the famous chair, including a visiting prince who paid a suitably princely sum – twenty guineas – for the seat. The other great attraction for the hackers was the mulberry tree. 'The mulberry-tree is the property of a carpenter who forms it into a number of little articles, such as tooth-pick cases, goblets, snuff-boxes etc. If we may judge by the sale of these things, a forest of mulberry-trees would hardly supply the wood that has already been sold.' The credibility of the souvenirs suffered a sad blow on the day the tree itself suffered a sadder – it was chopped down by the owner because, he said, its branches were keeping the light away from his windows. The citizens were so incensed that the unhappy man was eventually forced to flee the town, but whether the wrath of the local population came from righteous indignation at the destruction of such a reminder of the great man or from anger at the loss of a profitable business is not recorded. Finally, here is Charles Moritz who added a wry note to the whole business, and surely his experience must have been repeated a hundred times over.

> We went to see Shakespeare's own house, which of all the houses in Stratford I think is now the worst, and one that made the least appearance. Yet, who would not be proud to be the owner of it? There now however lived in it only two old people who show it to strangers for a trifle, and what little they can earn thus is their chief income.
>
> Shakespeare's chair, in which he used to sit before the door, was so cut to pieces that it hardly looked like a chair; for every one that travels through Stratford cuts off a chip as a remembrance, which he carefully preserves and deems a precious relic. I also cut myself a piece of it, but reverencing Shakespeare as I do, I am almost ashamed to own to you it was so small that I have lost it.

So much for Shakespeare's Stratford. But what of the other towns that are popular with tourists today? How many of those were marked down on the eighteenth-century travellers' maps? In fact, a great many. The university city of Oxford is today filled with coach loads of tourists, and much the same was true two centuries ago. Indeed, Oxford was so popular that many writers with little new to add, followed the example of Stebbing Shaw and said little. 'In the evening we proceeded to Oxford, the sacred seat of the muses; the antiquity and particulars of which I shall not pretend to describe; the two universities are places so well known, and so full of matter for contemplation and description, that nothing less than a separate work can give an account adequate to their respective merits. I shall therefore pass this place over in silent veneration and only insert a few common observations on recent improvements in that noble city.' But there were always those willing to take the opportunity to pontificate on such well-loved themes as the appalling dissipation of the undergraduates and the general uselessness of university education.

> The expense of education, of rooms, of battels, is moderate enough; but the extra charges on parents for the dissipations arising from wine parties, excursions, unnecessary dress, etc render it impossible to maintain a son as a commoner for less than 150*l* or 200*l* per annum. Thus a degree will cost from 6 to 800*l*; and probably a situation of 40*l* a year, the bare interest of the money expended on his education, is all that a young man without patronage, will gain by a four year residence in Oxford. It is not thus in trade: its prospects are more certain, and its charges less.

And there was that other evergreen topic – the relative merits of Oxford and Cambridge. Each had its own supporters, and detractors. E. D. Clarke found Oxford to be an ill-organised jumble. 'In Oxford there seems what may be styled a *disease* of *buildings*.' But William Mavor was having none of that. 'While Oxford is one of the finest Gothic cities in the world, Cambridge sinks even below mediocrity.' Being Oxford locals – as, it must be confessed, was William Mavor – we present these opposing views without comment.

The other great attractions were the spas and watering places, where an excess of good living could hopefully be counteracted by the health giving waters. Of these, Bath stood almost unchallenged. Even when Defoe visited it in the 1720s it was decidedly popular and had already been taken over by the healthy hankering after enjoyment in place of the sick searching for cures.

> The bathing is made more a sport and a diversion, than a physical prescription for health; and the town is taken up in raffling, gameing, visiting, and in a word, all sorts of gallantry and levity.
> The whole time indeed is a round of the utmost diversion. In the morning you (supposing you to be

a young lady) are fetch'd in a close chair, dress'd in your bathing cloths, that is, stript to the smock, to the Cross-Bath. There the musick plays you into the bath, and the women that tend you, present you with a floating wooden dish, like a bason; in which the lady puts a handkerchief, and a nosegay, of late the snuff-box is added, and some patches; tho' the bath occasioning a little perspiration, the patches do not stick so kindly as they should.

Here the ladies and the gentlemen pretend to keep some distance, and each to their proper side, but frequently mingle here too, as in the Kings and Queens Bath, tho' not so often; and the place being but narrow, they converse freely, and talk, rally, make vows, and sometimes love; and having thus amus'd themselves an hour, or two, they call their chairs and return to their lodgings.

Such goings-on were not tolerated for long. Changes began in 1705 when Beau Nash visited Bath. He was only 29 years old, but already had a reputation as a high-living man about town. He was first attracted by the gaming tables, but found little in Bath to his taste. He suggested to the corporation that changes were needed and that he was the man to undertake them. The corporation, happy to find such a willing volunteer, agreed. Nash opened a subscription for an assembly room, hired musicians and laid down strict rules of conduct. He became the autocrat of Bath, and even royalty had to accept his rule. The fashionable flocked in. Nash made his money from gambling, and when laws were passed in 1740 banning games of chance his influence began to wane. But by then Bath was firmly established. It was unique. It had, as E. D. Clarke explained, everything.

Thus Bath may be said to afford a universal scope for everything that is desirable. The man of pleasure, may be here satiated with amusement; the philosopher, may analyze its salubrious springs; the antiquarian, may pursue his researches till he wearies himself with conjecture; the man of letters, will find ample repositories of genius; the poet, endless subjects to exercise his wit; the painter, may delineate the features of beauty, or portray the luxuriant variety of landscape; and, last of all, the dejected invalid, may restore to its wonted tenour the shattered system of a broken constitution, and, by rousing his debilitated nerves to their accustomed tone, revive his health and renovate his spirits.

Bath, however, was less a stopping off place for travellers than a way of life, so that in a sense it can hardly be said to form part of a tourist's itinerary. Other spas, though less significant than Bath, had their champions. Matlock must hold pride of place, for it served a dual role as spa and as a centre for exploring the Derbyshire Peak District. Further north, in Yorkshire, Harrogate was just beginning to gain popularity. Like Matlock, it was well situated as a centre for the observation of picturesque scenery. Besides exploring the countryside, those with a strong stomach – and strong nose – could always try the water from the springs. Prince Pückler-Muskau, after declaring that though Harrogate was unfashionable it was a very attractive town, went on to do just that. The result was not as anticipated. 'The sulpherous water I drank today has made me so ill that I cannot leave my room.'

Spa water was not the only water considered to have beneficial effects; similar claims were made for sea water, and so the seaside resort was added to the list of places to be visited. Jane Austen's description of the delights of Lyme Regis could almost as easily describe the pleasures a modern visitor might find on a visit. 'The remarkable situation of the town, the principal street almost hurrying into the water, the walk to the Cobb, skirting round the pleasant little bay, which in the season is animated with bathing machines and company, the Cobb itself, its old wonders and new improvements, with the very beautiful line of cliffs stretching out to the east of the town, are what the stranger's eye will seek; and a very strange stranger it must be, who does not see charms in the immediate environs of Lyme, to make him wish to know it better.' These are indeed the charms we still see, but for most Georgians the aim of a seaside visit was not just to admire the scenery, and the life of the seaside resort was very different from that of today.

William Hutton, whom we last met at York, set out for Scarborough in 1803 with the principal object of helping his daughter recover from a long illness. It was by no means cheap staying in the town. 'The accommodations we found were of three sorts: to take a furnished house, if a family arrived, which may be done from 6 to 10 guineas a week; or to take apartments in a family, and find food and servants yourself, or board and lodge in a family at a stated price. We chose the last. The terms were, 25 shillings a week each, for my daughter and I, exclusive of tea and liquors, and ten shillings each for a bed. The servant half, or seventeen shillings and sixpence, and the same sum for the horse, including corn.' Once settled in, the ladies were kept busy with harmless, if dull sounding, occupations – so far as one can tell they did little more than go down to the sea shore to make collections of seaweed and shells. There was a little riding on horseback and the ritual drinking of the spa water. But then, as another traveller noted, Scarborough was not exactly brimful of entertainments for the visitor if he or she chanced to grow tired of scenery and seaweed. 'The romantic situation of Scarborough renders it a pleasing view, to travellers who have no eye to the amusements of the place. It is destitute of public buildings that attract attention: even the rendezvous of pleasure, the long-rooms, are paltry holes; by no means worthy the resort of so much good company as this place boasts.' On the other hand, it was a great improvement on nearby Whitby, which earned this rebuke from the Duke of Rutland. 'It is a dirty town, and if an opinion may be taken from the regulations adopted as necessary and requisite in the assembly rooms, it does not possess a very civilized set of inhabitants. The two first rules had for their object, the preservation of proper order amongst the female part of the society; – they were as follows:

RULE I. There will be no swearing among the Ladies.
    II. No lady shall be allowed to call for Gin before ten o'clock.'

Hutton's stay in Scarborough did succeed in its main object and he was able to chart his daughter's recovery. 'Almost 4 weeks elapsed before any change was apparent, when her breathing, activity and strength began gradually to return; and Nature seemed approaching toward her former tone.' Hutton also had the unexpected pleasure of seeing the fleets go by, and an amazing sight it must have been – and an encouraging one, for a country at war. 'In the morning of July the 4th 1803, I saw 200 sail from Newcastle towards the South: a fleet which took two or three hours to pass. They were unguarded, though at war with France. In the evening, I saw the Baltic fleet move towards the North; what number I cannot tell, but with a glass, we counted 198 at a view, which, to a landman like myself, was a pleasing sight. The sea seemed inhabited as much as the land.' Not the sort of thing one could count on seeing, but what a truly splendid sight it must have made – hundreds of ships under full sail. A seaside delight that we, alas, will never know.

Hutton's daughter was really fortunate in her convalescence, for Scarborough was noted for its mineral waters and she was spared the fate of many a sick girl sent to the seaside of actually having to drink the sea water itself. It was certainly an age with a good deal of faith in the medicinal properties of sea water. At Bournemouth, enough money was raised by public subscription to open a special infirmary for treating sufferers from all manner of unlikely complaints with the miraculous liquid. There was absolutely no evidence to support the idea that sea water was good for the patients – the main advantages the takers of the water obtained probably came from fresh air and exercise. On the other hand, sea water was at least preferable to the normal eighteenth-century remedies of repeated bleedings and purgatives, with the richer and more 'fortunate' invalids benefiting from such splendidly modern treatments as galvanism or, more simply, violent electrical shocks.

Drinking sea water was an activity limited to the unfortunate few – the rest made do with the more conventional procedure of bathing in it. This was the age of the bathing machines, such as those at Aberystwyth which were 'of the usual form, constructed of wood, topped in a pavilion shape, and running on four wheels. Three or four are allotted in one quarter to the ladies: and as many in another to the gentlemen.' So the ladies and gentlemen gathered at a discreet distance – none of that indecorous mingling Defoe had noted at Bath – and clambered into their little wooden boxes. When everyone was safely stowed away to change, the machines were rolled out into the sea, so that the bathers could slip safely from changing room to water without risk of being seen. Not that they were expected actually to enjoy bathing – it was considered strictly medicinal. Sukey Wedgwood, daughter of the famous potter, wrote this description of her first encounter with the sea: 'I only drank the salt water one day before I *ventured* into the open sea which I did this morning & very courageously too considering what a great coward I am – the water is not near so cold as our bath & not very salt 'tho enough so to make me shut my mouth a little closer tomorrow.'

Heaven only knows what the Georgians would have made of a modern beach scene, though one does get a glimmering from their comments on those beaches where the usually strict standards were lacking. Prince Pückler-Muskau noted with horror that at Bangor 'Every body may jump into the sea who like it'. As this was clearly not an activity in which a gentleman, let alone a prince, could be expected to join, he had to find some other means of taking to the water. In the event, that proved almost as alarming. 'The artificial arrangements for the purpose are reduced to the private tub-establishment of one old woman, who lives in a wretched hovel on the shore; and if an order is given an hour before, heats the sea water in pots and kettles on her hearth, and proceeds "sans façon", to undress and afterwards to rub down and dress again any stranger who may come unprovided with a servant.' Had the prince stayed in Wales longer and enquired more thoroughly, he would have found an even more astonishing lack of inhibition. William Mavor did enquire and discovered a surprising local custom.

> The natives of both sexes among the mountains on the sea coast of Cardiganshire and probably in other places, are much addicted to sea-bathing, during the light summer nights. The manner of their collecting together, is by blowing horns the whole way as they advance towards the deep. When arrived on the beach, they strip, and take a promiscuous plunge without any ceremony. This kind of ablution is generally performed on Saturdays, in order that they may enjoy rest the next day. It is generally daylight before they return to their houses, and the noise they make is sure to disturb those who are not engaged in these aquatic orgies.

Aquatic orgies! Not at all the sort of thing that the average tourist had in mind when he took his tentative dip into the ocean in the hope of curing his gout. The whole attitude of the tourists was so very different from that of the locals – fresh air, salt water and exercise were considered safe only if taken in very small doses. The novels of the period are full of heroines who are forced to bed after a ten-minute walk in the rain, while tripping over a clump of grass is sufficient to bring them to death's door – a midnight bathe, even if such a thing could have been considered, would have finished them off for sure. It was to be a good long while before the idea of bathing for pleasure was generally accepted, and in the meantime the visitors went on with their shell collecting, walks and picnics and did the rounds of assembly rooms and circulating libraries.

Georgian tourist or modern tourist, tastes seem much the same: stately homes, antique ruins, picturesque towns and seaside resorts are as popular now as then. Of course the Georgian visitors to stately homes went as equals, expecting to be admitted as of right, rather than as tourists, allowed under sufferance to satisfy an economic necessity. Once there, our predecessors' interests were very similar to our own – they wandered around house and grounds, looked at the pictures on the walls and eyed the architecture. We have been conditioned to accept all great houses as necessarily beautiful, but to the tourists of that time, they were often not old buildings but brand new, and it was in those terms that they were criticised. It is easy to forget that all architecture was modern architecture once. Like ourselves, these earlier tourists hunted for souvenirs, and like us, complained that they were not getting value for money. Their souvenir hunting was not necessarily of a type that would be encouraged today: the authorities would take a dim view of anyone emulating one traveller who took a fancy to some medieval stained glass and proceeded to hack out and cart away the faces of five saints. Differences are perhaps most marked at the seaside. Today, we lie on beaches trying to get the maximum sunshine to the maximum area of skin. A young lady of two centuries ago who was unwise enough to venture onto the shore without her sun hat would be expected at best to suffer a nervous headache, at worst to be prostrate for a fortnight. Yet, whatever the differences in attitudes, the places themselves are all those that we would expect to find in the tourist map of today. There was, however, another group of popular attractions for which there are no modern equivalents.

4

A Changing World

THE Lake District is grand, but surely the Alps are grander? The Roman remains at York are fine, but can they really compare with the majestic ruins of Greece or Italy? The British traveller might well have to agree that his native attractions came off second best in competition with such Continental rivals, but in one area at least eighteenth-century Britain stood triumphantly alone. Britain was the only country to be going through that great social and economic upheaval we know as the Industrial Revolution. It was a source of pride to the local traveller, quite astonishing to the visitor from over-seas. Faujas St-Fond's views may have been coloured by religious bigotry, but the differences he noted between the new industrial scenes in Britain and those of continental Europe were real enough.

This beautiful river the Tyne, is rendered highly interesting by the number and variety of the manu-factures carried on upon its banks. On one hand are seen brick-fields, potteries, glass-houses and chymical works for making ceruse, minium, vitriol etc., on the other manufactories in iron, tin and every kind of metal; machines for making brass-wire, plate-metal, etc.

This multitude of establishments rising opposite to one another, diffuses everywhere so much activity and life, if I may use the expression, that the eye is agreeably astonished in contemplating such a mag-nificent picture. Humanity rejoices to see so many useful men finding ease and happiness in a labour which contributes, at the same time, to the comforts and enjoyments of others; and in the last result, to the prosperity of the government, which watches over the safety of all.

Compare this honourable industry with that disgraceful indolence and disgusting misery which is to be seen in Roman Catholic countries, where pernicious laws permit a great portion of the population to be buried in monastic institutions, and it will soon be discovered how much government and religion influence the happiness of mankind.

Today we regard holidays as an opportunity to get away from the clamour and noise of industrial life – not so the Georgian travellers. For them, the huge expansion of industry was new and exciting, a source of great wonder. Yet they soon found that a way of fitting the new industry into existing tourist slots. There was, for example, an industrial picturesque to place alongside the more familiar rural picturesque: accustomed to knocking on doors and demanding to see great houses, the tourists found little difficulty in making a minor adjustment and soon began knocking on other doors and demanding to see great factories. It is hard to imagine visiting Cowley or spending a day watching a motorway construction unit as a holiday treat, but then the industrial world is our everyday world; all sense of novelty has gone. We are very unlikely ever again to experience the awed amazement of the early travellers who were present at the birth of the first industrial society.

The new roads that the tourists travelled represented one aspect of the industrial revolution – the improvement in transport – but they were nothing like as exciting as the new canals. When the Duke of Bridgewater built the country's first canal in 1761, people travelled from all over Britain to see its greatest wonder – the Barton aqueduct. Here was something new: a river in the air, water passing over water. It was even declared by some pious locals to be unnatural, if not an actual blasphemy. An anonymous tourist catches the mood perfectly in this description.

'Tis not long since I viewed the artificial curiosities of London, and now have seen the natural wonders of the Peak; but none of them have given me so much pleasure as I now receive in surveying the Duke of Bridgewater's navigation in this county. His projector, the ingenious Mr Brindley, has indeed made such improvements in this way, as are truly astonishing. At Barton bridge he has erected a navigable canal in the air; for it is as high as the tops of trees. Whilst I was surveying it with a mixture of wonder and delight, four barges passed me in the space of about three minutes, two of them being chained together, and dragged by two horses, who went on the terras of the canal, whereon, I must own, I durst hardly venture to walk, as I almost trembled to behold the large river Irwell underneath me, across which this navigation is carried by a bridge, which contains upon it the canal of water, with the barges in it, drawn by horses, which walk upon the battlements of this extraordinary bridge.

Barton was the tourists' favourite, but bolder souls could go on to Worsley where the canal went underground into the Duke's coal mines. Boats were hauled by handrails right up to the coal face, and Henry Skrine was one of those who made the trip. 'I went as far as the two first pits in a boat ferried by a true resemblance of Charon, through this terrestrial Acheron, but the damps prevailed so much, that my conductor prevented my penetrating further into these regions of sulphur and inflammability.'

The fuse was lit for a vast explosion of energy. During the next half century quite literally thousands of miles of canal were constructed, and in the process new wonders appeared that quite overshadowed the once miraculous-seeming, but really quite modest, aqueduct at Barton.

Later engineers built bigger and better, and the pinnacle of achievement came with the construction of the great aqueduct of Pontcysyllte, which carries the Ellesmere Canal 120 feet above the River Dee near Llangollen. Small wonder that William Mavor – even if he did raise it in his comments by an extra fifty feet – should have described it as one of 'the most stupendous works of art that ever was accomplished by man'. When Mavor went to see it, the aqueduct had just been completed, but the water was not yet in, so he missed the real excitement of travelling across by boat. For once, the modern traveller has the advantage over his predecessor, for the great thing about Pontcysyllte is that the metal plates of the aqueduct's side are actually below the gunwales of the boat, and the boatman has the distinctly eerie sensation of being suspended in space more than a hundred feet above the ground. What the gentleman who 'hardly durst' walk over the wide, low aqueduct at Barton would have made of Pontcysyllte one cannot imagine.

At the opposite extreme to the airy passage by aqueduct was a journey through one of the low, dark tunnels. The first of these, at Harecastle on the Trent and Mersey Canal, was almost two miles long, and the work of driving it through the hillside took eleven years to complete. But when it was finally finished, a proud company laid on pleasure boats to take visitors through the workings. During construction, the diggers had come across coal, and side passages led off to the various workings, so that away from the main channel there was a good deal of activity. The Rev. Stebbing Shaw took the trip, and at first found it quite idyllic.

I visited this tunnel about the year 1770, soon after it was finished, when pleasure boats were then kept for the purpose of exhibiting this great wonder; the impression it made on my mind, is still very fresh. The procession was solemn; some enlivened this scene with a band of musick, but we had none; as we entered far, the light of candles was necessary, and

about half-way, the view back upon the mouth, was
like the glimmering of a star, very beautiful.

He may not have realised just how fortunate he was in
not having a band playing in a tunnel a mere nine feet
wide. The music would, in any case, have had to compete
with other sounds: 'The various voices of the workmen
from the mines, &c., were rude and awful, and to be
present at their quarrels, which sometimes happen when
they meet, and battle for a passage, must resemble greatly
the ideas we may form of the regions of Pluto.'

The poet Robert Southey went on a tour of Scotland
which included a visit to the works on the Caledonian
Canal. For once, one can be reasonably certain that when
facts and figures are quoted they are accurate since his
companion on the journey was the chief engineer of the
canal, Thomas Telford. Nevertheless, Southey was as
prone as any other tourist of his day to wild enthusiasms.
Certainly the canal, which was designed to take ocean
going vessels rather than the more humble barge or
narrow boat, was impressive, and the great flight of
locks near Fort William known as Neptune's Staircase
is spectacular, but even the most ardent canal enthusiast
might find it difficult to accept Southey's verdict.

We landed close to the Sea-lock; which was full, and
the water running over; a sloop was lying in the fine
basin above; and the canal was full as far as the Staircase, a name given to the eight successive locks. Six
of these were full and overflowing; and when we drew
near enough to see persons walking over the lock-
gates, it had more the effect of a scene in a panto-
mime, than anything in real life. The rise from lock
to lock is eight feet, 64 therefore in all; the length of
the locks, including the gates and abutments at both
ends, 500 yards – the greatest piece of such masonry
in the world, and the greatest work of its kind,
beyond all comparison.

A panorama painted from this place would include
the highest mountain in Great Britain, and its

greatest work of art. That work is one of which the magnitude and importance become apparent when considered in relation to natural objects. The Pyramids would appear insignificant in such a situation, for in them we would perceive only a vain attempt to vie with greater things. But here we see the powers of nature brought to act upon a great scale, in subservience to the purposes of man: one river created, another (and that a huge mountain stream) shouldered out of its place, and art and order assuming a character of sublimity.

The Caledonian was one of the last of Britain's canals, and when Southey visited it he found evidence of the new technology. There were still thousands of labourers at work with shovels and wheelbarrows, but their efforts were aided by such wonders of the modern age as a steam dredger that could shift eight hundred tons a day. Southey filled page after page of his notebooks with technical details, which also convey his sense of awe at the vastness of the work and the immensity of the achievement. To find such scenes where 'men appeared in the proportion of emmets to an ant-hill' in a remote region of the Scottish highlands added to the feeling that what was being seen was indeed man in the process of changing the whole face of nature.

Once complete, the canals offered a pleasant alternative to the road as a means of travel, having the great advantage of being entirely free from ruts and humps. The passengers were assured of a smooth ride, provided the boatman did not steer into the bank and provided they remembered to duck at the low bridges. The canal boat offered comforts not available to the stage-coach traveller on his journey. The Manchester to Warrington boat, for example, boasted 'a coffee-room at the head, from whence wines, &c are sold out by the Captain's wife.' It was not a good idea for the passenger to avail himself too freely of the wines on the Duke of Bridgewater's boats, as the boatmen were under strict instructions to

turn off any passengers who misbehaved. For those dis-
inclined to view the scenery, or risk a long, humiliating
walk down the towpath, there were newspapers on sale.
Still, there were always a few who found the canals too
peaceful, the boats too slow, and who looked for a little
more excitement in their lives. For them, there was the
opportunity to see a rather more exhilarating form of
transport by visiting South Wales. There the various
industrial concerns were often linked to each other and to
the canals by tramways – early railways on which trucks
were pulled by horses. Unlike the modern railways, they
were often remarkably steep, the trucks being allowed to
run downhill and being winched back up. The Duke of
Rutland visited one of these early railways when he
stopped off to see the Brecon and Abergavenny Canal.

In the middle of this glen, are some iron works
belonging to a Mr. Frere; and farther still, some coal
works belonging to Mr. Kendal himself, which he
rents of the Duke of Beaufort. This rail-road is
adapted to the size of the waggons, or carts, which
convey the coal to the canal. On each side is an iron
groove, which extends the whole length of the road,
and on which the wheels (four or six in number)
run. They are so contrived as to run downwards the
whole way (sometimes for the extent of some miles)
from the works; so that when laden, they require no
horses to draw them down. Indeed they acquire so
great a degree of velocity in their descent, that a
man is forced to walk or run behind the cart, with a
kind of rudder or pole affixed to the hind-wheel,
which he locks up when it proceeds too fast. Should
this pole break (which it sometimes does) the waggon
flies away, and overturns everything it meets. Of
course, any one who is coming up the road, is in
imminent danger, unless he can by any means get
out of the way; which is very difficult, as the road is
narrow, and runs along a precipice. Last year, Mr.
Frere, the proprietor of the iron works, was returning

from London, and going along the rail-road in a
post-chaise, when about a hundred yards from him,
he saw one of those waggons coming down upon him
with astonishing velocity. He could not possibly get
out of the way, and must have been crushed to pieces,
if fortunately the waggon had not broken over the
iron groove, which had hitherto kept it in the track,
and run forcibly up an ash-tree by the side of the road,
in the branches of which it literally stuck, and thus
saved him from immediate destruction.

Such accounts might help to explain why fewer tourists
visited the tramways than the canals.

The transport system was built to serve the new
industries, and had many civil engineering triumphs to
its credit, but the main interest lay with the industries
themselves. This interest was not necessarily in proportion to the importance of a particular development. What
really attracted was the spectacle of mighty machines, the
power of steam, the awesome vision of flames and
billowing smoke – or, to put it another way, the tourists
liked their industries to be grandly picturesque. There
were few more awesomely magnificent than the rapidly
developing metal industries. The blast furnaces where
iron was made, the forges where it was shaped both came
in for regular comment. The Duke of Rutland, not a
writer usually much given to extravagant language was
quite overcome by his visit to the famous Dowlais iron
works at Merthyr Tydfil, and whatever his account might
lack in technical expertise it more than makes up for by
recreating the sense of excitement he felt as he got nearer
to the works.

As we approached them, the effect was grand and
sublime beyond all description. The fires from the
furnaces were bursting forth in the darkness of the
night, and every moment we saw as it appeared, a
red-hot bar of iron walking towards us, the man who
carried it not being visible. In the perspective, we
could see numbers of Vulcans dragging about pigs

of iron just taken from the furnaces, (the fires of which would dazzle the strongest eyes) and pursuing their different operations, while their grimly figures, and gloomy visages, were visible by the light of the forges. We saw them running about in all directions through the door-ways of the buildings, some of them hammering others rolling the iron, while the regular thumps of a great hammer, which we heard far off, before we came near the works, and gradually increased to a thundering noise as we approached, completed the grandeur of the scene. I never saw anything that gave me more the idea of the infernal regions.

An equally ecstatic reaction came from E. D. Clarke who visited Swansea, where the copper ore from Devon and Cornwall was smelted. 'One beautiful spectacle, however, we had the luck to meet with on our return to Swansea, and it came the more grateful, as it was unexpected. This arose from the smelting houses, which in the middle of a heavy rain, and a dark night, displayed such a glorious light, and so many beautiful colours from their ashes which lay on each side of the road, that I should not have regretted being wet through, if it was for the pleasure of seeing these alone.'

The furnaces, the glare of the flames and the hot metal were indeed astonishing, and as many of these early industries were set in wild and open countryside it must have seemed as though man was competing directly with nature in producing magnificent effects. That nature might be losing out in this competition did not occur to the onlookers, so that we find William Coxe praising the 'picturesque' iron works at Blaenavon in South Wales, with a special word of commendation for the way in which the effect was heightened 'by the volumes of black smoke emitted by the furnaces'.

Sometimes, the picturesque effects of industry could be found right next to the more conventional beauty spots. Visitors crowded to see Tintern Abbey and quite a few stayed on to view the Tintern iron works, and found nothing odd in this juxtaposition. Prince Pückler-Muskau, who had waxed poetic over the abbey became, if anything, even more enthusiastic when he came to describe the iron works. 'Fires gleam in red, blue, and yellow flames, and blaze up through lofty chimneys, where they assume at times the form of huge glowing flowers . . .' The works were powered by 'an immense water wheel . . . The frightful noise when it was first set going, the furnaces around vomiting fire, the red-hot iron, and the half-naked black figures brandishing hammers and other ponderous instruments, and throwing around the red hissing masses, formed an admirable representation of Vulcan's smithy.' There are not many today who would mourn the passing of industry from the beautiful, wooded Wye valley, or miss the smoke and flames, however picturesque.

The bigger the works, the greater the attraction: Dowlais, where the owner Mr Crayshaw claimed that 'at present he made more iron than probably any person in the world'. Carron, in Scotland, famous for the carronades, short, large-bore cannon that were put to use at Trafalgar and Waterloo; visitors were made welcome here but were kept well away from the section of the works where they carried out the secret boring process. Most important of all was Coalbrookdale in Shropshire, where the modern iron industry was born. It was here in 1709 that Abraham Darby first used coke to smelt iron, and it was here just over half a century later that the world's first iron bridge was built, as great a wonder as the aqueduct at Barton. Henry Skrine wrote: 'We made a precipitate descent to the romantic scene of Colebrookdale, where the river, winding between a variety of high wooded hills, opposite to the forges of Borseley, is crossed by a bridge of one arch, 100 feet in length and formed entirely of cast iron with strong stone abutments which presents at once a striking effect in landscape, and a stupendous specimen of the powers of mechanism.' Stupendous indeed, and one of the very few industrial sites that is still a tourist attraction today.

Two themes soon emerge from the many accounts of

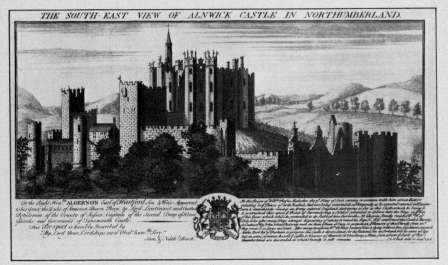

Then, as now, stately homes were much visited: *above* the recently renovated Alnwick Castle, Northumberland; but not all of them were admired. Willersley Castle, *·below* built by the industrialist, Sir Richard Arkwright, was described as 'the house of an overseer surveying the works.'

Some visitors added sketches to their notes of the houses they visited: *above* a house at Redlands, near Bristol, and *below* some picturesque fragments.

Bath became the fashionable centre of Georgian Britain. In the late seventeenth century, this was far from the case, when such outrageous behaviour as mixed bathing was permitted. A century later (*below*) Bath was gaining a new elegance: the Crescent.

Shakespeare's birthplace (*above*) was immensely popular,
and the seaside, too, was beginning to attract visitors.
below A blustery day on the beach at Barmouth.

industry: first the classical. Tourists usually managed to
squeeze in a classical allusion when describing the scenes
they had witnessed. An anonymous tourist looking at
workers on the Bridgewater Canal observed that 'the
whole posse appeared, as I conceive did that of the Tyrians,
when they wanted houses to put their heads in and were
building Carthage,' which is colourful but unlikely. We
may not know much about eighteenth-century navvies,
but it is fairly safe to assume that they were very little
like ancient Carthaginians. It is rare indeed to come
across a description of a blast furnace at work that does
not contain some such phrase as this of St-Fond's, used to
describe Carron: 'One doubts whether he is at the foot of
a volcano in actual eruption, or whether he has been
transported by some magical effect to the brink of the
cavern, where Vulcan and his Cyclops are occupied in
preparing thunderbolts.' By the time one has reached the
twelfth furnace description and been twelve times accosted
by Vulcan, one begins to long for a traveller who has
somehow managed to miss out on a classical education.
And this brings us to the second theme: the sense the
travellers had of seeing great changes, so great that it
was the most natural thing in the world to compare the
powers of the new machines with those supernatural
powers that shaped and reshaped the earth in the mytholo-
gies of Greece and Rome. It must have seemed that nothing
was impossible to the new gods of power, and that there
was no part of nature that man could not conquer.

This battle with nature was seen at its most dramatic
in man's attempt to wrest from the ground the raw
materials for his new industry. Incredible though it may
seem to us, the tourists' curiosity even took them down
the new, deep mines, though it must be confessed that this
remained a minority interest, and those who did go down
found the experience less than enjoyable. Nevertheless,
mining had its own aura of romance and, as R. J. Sullivan
put it – 'to have been at Newcastle, and men of curiosity
too, without seeing a coal-pit, would have been a sin of the
most unpardonable nature.' There was as much interest

in the tin and copper mines of the West Country as in the northern coal mines, and Clarke ventured down the Poldeis mine, near Truro.

> At about eighty fathoms depth we came to a vein of copper ore, where two sorry wretches were busied in the process of their miserable employment with hardly room to move their bodies; in sulphureous air, wet to the skin, and buried in the solid rock, these poor devils live and work for a pittance barely sufficient to keep them alive; pecking out the hard core by the glimmering of a small candle, whose scattered rays will hardly penetrate the thick darkness of the place. Those who live on earth in affluence, and are continually murmuring for additional comforts, would surely, if they saw these scenes, be happy with what they have.

Clarke kept going, even when the passageways became so low that he was forced to crawl on hands and knees, and there was the damp to add to his discomfort. By the end of the trip, he was soaked to the skin but he did at least have the consolation of knowing that his investigation of a mine had been a thorough one and at the end he could say, like the man banging his head against a brick wall – it's wonderful when you stop. 'It is impossible to describe the luxury one feels in breathing again the fresh air and washing with cold water, after these subterraneous excursions. The heat of a mine is excessive, and the deeper you go, the warmer becomes the air. The miners are quite naked when engaged at their work and they told me the change of climate, and the revolutions of winter and summer, were not to be perceived at that great depth.'

Clarke became something of an expert on mine workings, and was able to offer advice on which mines were most suitable for the casual visitor. He did not, however, go into some of the more unpalatable details, unlike the anonymous tourist who provided this alarming commentary on the clothes the intrepid explorer was required to wear. 'The cloaths they give you are as greasy as sweat can make them, smell abominably, and are often stocked with a republic of creepers.' For all that, the experience could be worth the trouble, and Clarke's description of his own personal favourite, the salt mine at Northwich, is enough to tempt anyone who could bring himself to make the initial descent.

The method of descent is by a bucket, through a perpendicular shaft, by which you are conducted into the very heart of the mine. Of the different subterraneous abodes I had visited, I found this by far the most agreeable that I ever saw. Here, without encountering the difficulties resulting from broken ladders, slippery precipices, horrid chasms, dismal dungeons, where one half of our bodies was soaked in water and the other exposed to the suffocating fumes of sulphur, we were introduced to a spectacle at once beautiful and surprising. Innumerable candles dispersed up and down the different parts of a vast glittering cavern, displayed a most pleasing scene; it resembles an illuminated grotto of transparent rockwork: the impression it affords at first entering it, is not unlike that which a stranger feels at being admitted to Vauxhall. The salt is separated from the main rock in large bodies by gunpowder: this process is conducted after a similar method to that which we saw practised in the coalmines. The workmen call it *making a blast*, and they were kind enough to fire one for our amusement, which seemed to shake the very earth itself. The roof of these immense caverns is supported by monstrous pillars of the salt rock, which are left in the course of working the mine safely for this purpose. The great cleanliness of these places might induce even the most timid female if she has curiosity enough, to descend and explore these regions of wonder. A lady might safely venture her person and apparel to the care of these sturdy miners, even though bedecked in all the splendour of a birthday suit.

It was possible to see men extract the raw materials from the earth without having to climb slippery ladders, be lowered in a bucket or crawl down dripping passage-ways. One could, for example, visit a slate quarry, though even that could not be described as an activity entirely devoid of risk. Prince Pückler-Muskau went to see such a quarry in Snowdonia, and his account is marvellously graphic, full of incident and detail.

> In order to reach a remote part of the works, where they were then blasting rocks with gunpowder, – a process which I had a great desire to see, – I was obliged to lie down in one of the little iron waggons which serve for the conveyance of the slate, and are drawn by means of a windlass through a gallery hewn in solid rock, only four feet in height, four hundred paces in length, and pitch dark. It is a most disagree-able sensation to be dragged through this narrow passage at full speed, and in Egyptian darkness, after having had ample opportunity of seeing at the entrance the thousand abrupt jagged projections by which one is surrounded. Few strangers make the experiment, spite of the tranquillizing assurances of the guide who rides before. It is impossible to get rid of the idea that if one came in contact with any of these salient points, one would, in all probability, make one's egress without a head. After passing through this gallery, I had to walk along a path at the edge of the precipice, only two feet wide, and without any railing or defence; then to pass through a second low cavern.

If few travellers made this alarming excursion, then they were the losers, for the Prince found himself faced with a scene which was 'fearfully magnificent' and more than repaid the risks of getting there.

> It was like a subterranean world! Above the blasted walls of slate, smooth as a mirror and several hundred feet high, scarcely enough of the blue heaven was visible to enable me to distinguish mid-day from

twilight. The ground on which we stood was likewise blasted rock; just in the middle was a deep cleft six or eight feet wide. Some children of the workmen were amusing themselves in leaping across this chasm for a few pence. The perpendicular sides were hung with men, who looked like dark birds, striking the rock with their long picks, and throwing down masses of slate which fell with a sharp and clattering sound. But on a sudden the whole mountain seemed to totter, loud cries of warning re-echoed from various points, – the mine was sprung. A large mass of rock loosened itself slowly and majestically from above, fell down with a mighty plunge, and while dust and splinters darkened the air like smoke, the thunder rang round in wild echoes. These operations, which are of almost daily necessity in one part or other of the quarry, are so dangerous, that, according to the statement of the overseer himself, they calculate on an average of an hundred and fifty men wounded, and seven or eight killed in a year.

The management, however, took the view – common enough at that time – that such accidents were not their concern.

The overseer assured me that half these accidents were owing to the indifference of the men, who are too careless to remove in time, and to a sufficient distance, though at every explosion they have full warning given them. The slate invariably splits in sharp-edged flakes, so that an inconsiderable piece thrown to a great distance is often sufficient to cut a man's hand, leg, or even head, clean off. On one occasion this last frightful accident, as I was assured, actually happened.

The Prince actually met a funeral procession while visiting the works, a macabre confirmation of the overseer's appalling statistics.

But of all the mining sites in the country, far and away the most popular with the tourists was the Parys Mountain in Anglesey. It was discovered in the late eighteenth century that a large part of the mountain was not made up of the usual rock, but was virtually one solid lump of copper ore. No need here to dig deep pits, all the miners needed to do was hack away pieces of the mountain, which they did until it resembled a gigantic Gruyère cheese. It must have been an astonishing sight, and it is no surprise to find the tourists crowding in to see this modern miracle. It was a scene of spectacular industry, and spectacular devastation. 'The external aspect of the hill is extremely rude and rises into enormous rocks of coarse, white quartz. The ore is lodged in a bason, or hollow, and has on one side a small lake, on whose waters distasteful as those of *Avernus* no bird is known to alight. The whole aspect of this tract has, by the mineral operations, assumed a most savage appearance. Suffocating fumes of the burning heaps of copper arise in all parts and extend their baleful influence for miles around. In the adjacent parts vegetation is nearly destroyed; even the mosses and lichens of the rocks have perished: and nothing seems capable of resisting the fumes but the purple Melic grass, which flourishes in abundance.' Thomas Pennant gives this description without comment. The details were elaborated on by Arthur Aikin who had 'a most interesting and entertaining day' visiting the site. 'We had no difficulty in distinguishing this celebrated mountain,' he wrote, without the least hint of irony, 'for it is perfectly barren from the summit to the plain below, not a single shrub, and hardly a blade of grass, being able to live in this sulphurous atmosphere.' The Georgian tourist may have found it enjoyable, but modern conservationists might take a different view. Two centuries later, Parys Mountain is still a sterile pile of rubble.

The civil engineers who built the canals produced the most impressive monuments to the new industrial age, mining and smelting the most spectacular processes, but the most important development lay with the textile industry. It was here that machines were taking over work that had once been done by hand and here that the new factories were being built to house these mechanical marvels.

The idea of a machine that could replace tens or even hundreds of people created a good deal of excitement. Here was real promise for a different sort of future: or, to look at it from another viewpoint, here was a threat to an established order, to the fixed patterns of society. John Byng went to Aysgarth to see the celebrated falls and also came across Nappa House, a fine mansion but rapidly collapsing into decay. He began to dream of repairing it. 'Retired from the world, a man might here enjoy fly-fishing and grouse shooting in the highest perfection.' But then he walked on and, rounding a bend, was confronted with the sight of a new cotton mill, and that 'completed the destruction of every rural thought'. From rustic day-dreams he turned to different thoughts. 'If men can thus start into riches; or if riches from trade are too easily procured, woe to us men of middling income, and settled revenue.' Nevertheless, he still went on to see Cromford, where Richard Arkwright had built his first water-powered cotton mill and set the whole process in motion. We have already heard his views on Arkwright's home. He was even less impressed with the new signs of industry. He saw the works and the workers and detested the whole scene. 'Every rural sound is sunk in the clamour of cotton works: and the simple peasant is changed into the impudent artisan.' He found Arkwright playing his favourite role of benevolent despot and noted down a poem that was pinned on the shop door, praising the man and his factory.

> *Come let us all here join in one,*
> *And thank him for all favours done;*
> *Let's thank him for all favours still*
> *Which he hath done besides the mill.*
>
> *Modistly drink liquor about,*
> *And see whose health you can find out;*
> *This will I chuse before the rest*
> *Sr Richard Arkwright is the best.*

A few more words I have to say
Success to Cromford's market day.

Hard to imagine a modern shop stewards' committee penning such lines to their managing director. Byng was having none of it. 'Sir Rd. Arkwright may have introduced much wealth into his family, and into the country; but, as a tourist, I execrate his schemes, which, having crept into every pastoral vale, have destroy'd the course and beauty of nature.'

Many of the tourists who went to Cromford came away disappointed, for Arkwright was a jealous guardian of his secrets, unwilling to allow strangers in to view the new machines. Consequently few travellers described the mill or the new town he had built for the workers, and mostly limited themselves to generalisations. They must often have shared Byng's dislike of the 'clamour' that had come to that particular pastoral vale, set right on the edge of the popular Derbyshire Peak District, but they certainly did not all share his dislike of trade. William Bray's eulogy may be tinged with condescension, but eulogy it is for all that. After commenting on the fact that the mill employed about two hundred, mainly children who 'work by turns, night and day', he turned his attention to the proprietor. 'Mr Arkwright was bred a barber, but true genius is superior to all difficulties, even those of education, and happily he found men of spirit to supply that money which he wanted to carry his schemes into execution. The undertaking amply repays them for their confidence.'

Most tourists were intrigued by the new machines and interested, if not fascinated, in the different processes by which wool or cotton was turned first to yarn and then to cloth. Stebbing Shaw saw weavers at work at Muxmore, near Stroud in Gloucestershire, and described the process of cloth finishing in some detail, but with little enthusiasm.

We saw every thing in its natural state and place: first the milling which by a long process of beating by hammers, worked with a water wheel, thickens the cloth after it is woven; next the wool is raised on its surface by the repeated use of cards made of teasels (a thistly plant produced in the west); after this it is sheared in a very pleasing manner by large instruments, whose motion is so confined as not to endanger cutting the cloth; thus they work it till it becomes remarkably fine. The other processes are too simple and common to mention. Upon the whole I think this business cannot be deemed so entertaining by many degrees to the eye of a stranger as that of the cotton, fustian etc in Derbyshire and Lancashire. These crowded hills and vales seem to have formed by nature a romantic and picturesque scenery, but this originality is greatly destroyed, like that of Matlock, by an abundance of modern buildings and ornaments.

Today, the mills of Stroud have mellowed with age and seem as picturesque to the modern traveller as they were brash to the Georgian tourist. Nevertheless, one can sympathise with the earlier generation who preferred their hills and dales uncluttered. Our own attitudes are not so very different from theirs. We too tend to applaud the idea of economic growth and the latest labour-saving inventions. We too demand new products from industry. Like them we prefer to see the factory itself set down outside someone else's back door. But the early travellers showed a greater curiosity, wanting to see all the changes for themselves. The task was made pleasant by the fact that so many of the mills were found in largely rural areas. It was easy insofar as the machines they went to see were mechanically quite simple and no expert knowledge was needed to follow their workings.

To visit a mill at Matlock or Stroud was one thing, to go and see the rapidly developing textile towns of the north west was another. No matter how the writer decked his description out with glowing phrases, in the end he said little more than that the main towns were big and getting bigger. 'An idea of the immense population of the country in the environs of Manchester burst upon the mind on a sudden, when we reached the summit of a hill about two miles without the town, where a prodigious champaign of country, was opened to us, watered by the Irwell, filled with works of art; mansions, villages, manufactories and that gigantic parent of the whole, the widely-spreading town of Manchester.' The Rev. Richard Warner did not pass on the information of just where he stood to get this view of Manchester, which is a pity, for a fellow cleric, the Rev. William MacRitchie complained that 'from no point have you a good view of Manchester. It is situated in a plain; and the country all round it is a plain.' Not very illuminating comments, perhaps, but then even the most naturally curious of tourists might balk at spending what was, after all, intended principally as a holiday, in an investigation of Manchester and its rapidly growing slums.

Other industrial centres had their own interests and attractions, especially the town which beyond all others seemed to epitomise the astonishing changes of the period, Birmingham. There has always been about it a sort of raw quality, a tendency to cock the snook at visitors, as if to say – all right, so I'm dirty and ugly, but just you look and see what I can do! It was the child of the industrial revolution, a precocious infant that grew at a phenomenal rate, happy to substitute sheer strength and size for grace and elegance. It was a bawling, demanding infant, that insisted on getting attention and got it. The travellers may have had differing views about Birmingham, but a surprisingly large number went there. It was a difficult place to ignore.

Many simply agreed with the bald statement of Prince Pückler-Muskau, that Birmingham was 'one of the most considerable and one of the ugliest towns in England'. They stayed just long enough to gaze with a sense of wonder at the size and complexity of the place, before succumbing to its ugliness and scampering off again. Some did not even stay that long but only noted, with Henry Wigstead, 'a confused mass of brick and tile

rubbish piled together, enveloped in an almost impenetrable smoky atmosphere'. They too left for sunnier and
healthier climes. A minority, however, saw in the grime of
Birmingham the beginnings of a new prosperity. At the
heart of this new wealth was the famous Soho foundry,
from which steam engines that were to transform industry
were sent out to the world. The Rev. Warner, who had
had little enough to say about Manchester, became
positively loquacious when he arrived at Soho to admire
the works and the home of its begetter.

> All the lesser stars were eclipsed by the extensive
> and elegant buildings that form the works of Messrs.
> Boulton and Watt, called Soho, which, together with
> the handsome mansion of the former gentleman,
> cover the declivities of a hill to the right of the turn-
> pike road at Handsworth, two miles from Birming-
> ham. The situation of the house is commanding, the
> disposition of the grounds tasty, and the manu-
> factories as striking for their neatness as magnificence;
> so that the different features of the place form a
> strikingly fine whole, both grand and beautiful; the
> more interesting, when we consider that it is entirely
> the creation of modern years, formed by the combined
> operation of taste, science and wealth, out of a
> desolate heath, inhabited only by a colony of rabbits.

He then continued by listing all the different items that
were manufactured at Soho, from the steam engines, for
which the names Boulton and Watt will always be
famous, right down to ornamental settings for jewellery.

Some tourists waxed as eloquent over the founders as
over the foundry. Faujas St-Fond was one of those who had
taken the trouble to acquire the necessary introductions,
and so was able to call on James Watt himself.

> I experienced much pleasure in visiting Mr Watt,
> whose extensive knowledge in Chymistry and the
> arts, rendered his conversation very interesting. His
> moral qualities and the engaging manner in which he

expressed his thoughts, daily encreased my respect for him. Mr Watt is a man of great conceptions. Nature has endowed him with a very vigorous mind and to his other excellent qualities he joins the mildest and most prepossessing manners which interest even at first sight . . . Mr Watt is so familiar with great inventions, possesses so much knowledge in the higher branches of machanics, and has brought the means of execution to so much perfection, that he may justly be ranked among the men who have chiefly contributed the present high prosperity to the useful arts and commerce of England.

There is no indication of what the Scotsman Watt would have thought of the last words of praise, nor do the records show what industrialists such as Boulton and Watt thought, in their turn, of the gentlemanly strangers who came in procession, knocking at their door, asking for tours of the works and expecting to hear words of industrial wisdom.

No two travellers' accounts of Birmingham coincide, largely because the town was changing so fast that a difference of a few years between visits made an astonishing difference to the landscape of the area. It was summed up in a popular song of the 1820s.

> *Full twenty years and more have passed*
> *Since I saw Brummagem.*
> *But I set out for home at last*
> *To good old Brummagem.*
> *But every place is altered so,*
> *There's hardly a single place I know.*
> *Which fills my heart with grief and woe*
> *For I can't find Brummagem.*

The other great centre for iron and steel manufacture was, of course, Sheffield. Arthur Young made extensive comments on the cutlery industry, and the hard and dangerous work of the grinders, but he was particularly taken with the forges where tools were shaped. 'I would advise you to view all the mills in town: among others do not forget the tilting-mill, which is a blacksmith's immense hammer in constant motion on an anvil, worked by water-wheels, and by the same power the bellows of a forge adjoining kept regularly blown: The force of this mechanism is prodigious; so great, that you cannot lay your hand upon a gate at three perches distance, without feeling a strong trembling motion, which is communicated to all the earth around.' But, however fascinating the tilt hammers or the nearby iron works, Mr Young, good agriculturalist that he was, could not resist adding: 'But what gave me much greater satisfaction than the iron works of Rotherham was the cabbage culture of Samuel Tucker.'

Boulton and Watt were famous names in the engineering industry. Equally famous in the potteries was the name of Josiah Wedgwood. The potteries were especially interesting to the tourists, for here were all the marks of a modern, innovating industrial process while the end product was the cosily domestic teapot or dinner plate. As Warner put it: 'It would surprize a modern fine lady, were I to tell her, that the cup from which she sips her tea had been through the hands of at least twenty-three workmen, before it met her lips.' It might indeed have surprised her but it is precisely this conjunction between the industrial and the domestic which makes pot works – Wedgwood's included – still popular with modern tourists. The overall scene of the potteries two centuries ago was hardly glamorous and Henry Skrine's romantically setting sun seems to have done something to light up his imagination.

This setting sun enlivened the whole scene, and gilded many distant objects with her declining rays as we descended to the smoky town of Newcastle under Lime. This place is situated on the side of a considerable hill, and descends rapidly into the vale. The busy air of a manufacturing town is visible in all its inhabitants, and its streets though wide and not

ill built are tinged deeply with the smoke of its
potteries. They cover all the adjacent country, and
extend to the village of Burslem at two miles
distance; near which Mr Wedgwood who may be
called the Prince of Potters has erected a palace-like
house close to his extensive works and given the
name of Etruria to the whole.

Not the most promising beginning perhaps. Smoke-
filled streets were becoming common enough in all
conscience, but here there was the comforting thought
that from such apparently gross beginnings something
fine would result. So it is that we find many tourists going
into quite elaborate details. Arthur Young who had
declined to give details of the works around Sheffield on
the grounds that it 'would require infinitely more time
than any one can suppose an *agricultural* observer could
give them,' found time in plenty for a long, close look at
the potteries. He showed at once how impressed he was
by the rapid expansion of the industry, almost losing his
main theme in a flurry of statistics. 'From Newcastle-
under-Lime I had the pleasure of viewing the Staffordshire
potteries at Burslem, and the neighbouring villages,
which have of late been carried on with such amazing
success. Here are 300 houses, which are calculated to
employ, upon an average, twenty hands each, or 6000 in
the whole; but if all the variety of people that work in
what may be called the preparation for the employment of
the immediate manufacturers, the total number cannot be
much short of 10,000 and it is increasing every day.'
From there Young went on to eulogise Wedgwood's
achievement in getting British earthenware on to the
markets of the world. Good Englishman that he was,
however, he clearly considered that all this trade with
foreigners might prove to be a mixed blessing. He dropped
dark and heavy hints of industrial espionage.

Large quantities are exported to Germany, Ireland,
Holland, Russia, Spain, the East Indies and much to
America: some of the finest sorts to France. A con-

siderable shop-keeper from the Pont-neuf at Paris was lately at Burslem, and bought a large quantity. It is possible, indeed, he came for more purposes than to buy; the French of that rank seldom travel for business which might be as well transacted by a single letter.

Young gave a long and detailed account of the different processes, from the preparation of raw materials to the finishing of the ware. One wonders just how many tourists really wanted the technical details, and how many were happy simply to acknowledge technology, approve the new wonders and go on their way to tell their friends what a marvellous age they lived in. But it is to writers like Young that we now turn to get an idea of the complexity, and the far-reaching implications of those industrial changes. Here is a short extract describing some of the processes leading up to the early stages of manufacture, the shaping of the pot.

> The common clay of the country is used for the early sorts; the finer kinds are made of clay from Devonshire and Dorsetshire, chiefly from Biddeford; but the flints from the Thames are all brought rough by sea, either to Liverpool or Hull and so by Burton . . . The flints are first ground in mills, and the clay prepared by breaking, washing and sifting, and then they are mixed in the requisite proportions. The flints are bought first by the people about the country; and by them burnt and ground, and sold to the manufacturers by the peck. It is then laid in large quantities on kilns, to evaporate the moisture; but this is a nice work, as it must not be too dry. Next it is beat with large wooden hammers and then is in order for throwing, and is moulded into the forms in which it is to remain.

All this just to start production of an everyday object like a gravy boat – all that long-distance transport, all that new heavy machinery – small wonder that Young and his contemporaries were fascinated and came knocking at Wedgwood's door, even though they were not certain of being asked inside. Young was quite right on the subject of spies, there was a very real fear of them, especially of spies from overseas. E. D. Clarke knew this and came prepared for disappointment.

> Here we visited Mr Wedgwood's curious and extensive pottery. I was fearful of being denied admittance to the works, as I knew that it is customary in these places to introduce strangers to what is called the store room and then dismiss them without any further trouble. This however was not the case here. We sent in our names to Mr Wedgwood, at his elegant little mansion which overlooks the Pottery, and received full permission from him to see the whole of the manufactory, except the rooms where the black and the new discovered blue ware is made and these they never shew to any one.

Clarke was lucky, even if he did miss seeing the two processes for which Wedgwood was famous, the basalt and the blue jasper. So was William Mavor at Worcester, where he learned the value of being a well-known writer. 'After breakfast', wrote Mavor, 'inspected the show rooms of Messrs Barr & Co., china manufacturers, who, on accidentally learning my name, shewed the most flattering attention and offered to conduct us over their manufactory.' Mavor declined, pleading lack of time, but gave Barr his plug for 'some beautiful and costly patterns of tea and table services of china'.

The tourists went on their way, eager for novelty, anxious to add their own accounts to the scores of others that described and evaluated the growth of industry. Whether they adopted an attitude of awe-struck horror, used the clichés of classicism or limited themselves to strict practical detail, they were giving expression to an authentic interest and assumed their readers would share it. Today, the introduction of an industrial scene in a travel book would require special explanation, an apology even. Two centuries ago, it seemed the most natural thing in the world. The processes were interesting, the scenes dramatic, but most importantly a new sort of world was in the making. Arthur Young put it perfectly:

> Such works, however their operations, causes, and consequences, have infinite merit, and do great credit to the talents of this very ingenious and useful man, who will have the merit, wherever he goes of *setting men to think.* Get rid of that dronish, sleepy, and stupid indifference, that lazy negligence, which enchains men in the exact path of their forefathers without enquiry, without thought, and without ambition, and you are sure of doing good. What trains of thought, what a spirit of exertion, what a mass and power of effort have sprung in every path of life, from the works of such men as Brindley, Watt, Priestley, Harrison, Arkwright . . . In what path of life can a man be found that will not animate his pursuit from seeing the steam-engine of Watt?

Young's question was, of course, rhetorical. There were certainly some among the aristocracy who would have answered that they preferred things just the way they were, thank you very much, but these could always be dismissed as a reactionary minority. Young could be confident that most of his readers would be nodding their heads in silent agreement, sharing the belief that Britain was standing at the beginning of a new and glorious age. But what of those who were not his readers for the very good reason they were unable to read at all? What of the poor who were required to do the work of the new age? We do not know their answer, for nobody asked them the question. But if the poor were not asked their view of the tourists, the tourists were not slow to give their view of the poor – and such views form a fascinating part of many travel books.

5

The Rich Man in his Castle, the Poor Man at his Gate

The rich man in his castle,
The poor man at his gate,
God made them high or lowly
And ordered their estate.

THE words of Mrs Alexander's famous hymn sum up very neatly the social philosophy of the majority of the tourists. The gulf between rich and poor was no accident, it was not even the result of conscious actions by individual men; rather it was all part of a divine order. The rich were rich because an all-wise providence had deemed that they should be rich. So with the poor. It was axiomatic that each section had in some way 'earned' its particular circumstances, and from this it followed, logically, that the poor must in some way be *bad*, else why had they not deserved better? Before looking at some of the ways in which this attitude affected the behaviour of the rich when faced by such of the poor as they chanced to meet along the way, we can take a look at the breadth of the gulf fixed between them. A very dramatic contrast can be found in the descriptions by Faujas St-Fond of meals in Scotland. First he described his own daily intake.

Breakfast (taken at ten o'clock)
    Plates of smoaked beef
    Cheese of the country and English cheese in trays
      of mahogany
    Fresh eggs

Salted herrings
Butter
Milk and cream
A sort of *bouillie* of oatmeal and water. In eating this
   bouillie each spoonful is plunged into a bason of
   cream, which is always beside it.
Milk worked up with the yolks of eggs, sugar and
   rum. This singular mixture is drank cold, and
   without being prepared by fire.
Currant jelly
Conserve of myrtle, a wild fruit that grows among
   the heath
Tea
Coffee
The three sorts of bread and Jamaica Rum

Dinner (at 4 p.m.)
1 A large dish of Scotch soup composed of broth of
   beef, mutton and sometimes fowl, mixed with a
   little oatmeal, onions, parsley and a considerable
   quantity of pease. Instead of slices of bread as in
   France, small slices of mutton and the giblets of
   fowls are thrown into this soup.
2 Pudding of bullock's blood and barley meal, seasoned
   with plenty of pepper and ginger
3 Excellent beef steaks broiled
4 Roasted mutton of the best quality
5 Potatoes done in the juice of the mutton
6 Sometimes heath-cocks, woodcocks or water-fowl
7 Cucumbers and ginger pickled with vinegar
8 Milk prepared in a variety of ways
9 Cream and Madeira wine
10 Pudding made of barley meal, cream and currants
   of Corinth, done up with suet
   Cheshire cheese, wines etc.
   After the toasts: tea, coffee, small tarts, butter and
   milk

That was not quite the end of the day's feasting. The
traveller could hardly be sent to bed hungry, so in the

evening he had his breakfast menu repeated all over again. The mind reels at the thought of smoked beef, herring and porridge with that extraordinary concoction of milk, rum and eggs as a nightcap, but the reaction of a modern stomach would surely be even more drastic. Then, with hardly a pause and no apparent sense of absurdity, Faujas St-Fond goes on to describe the food eaten by the Scottish poor. 'Their only sustenance consists of milk, potatoes, fish at certain times of the year, and oatmeal made into *bouillie* or cakes. Their beverage is pure water, and a few glassful's of whiskey on their festive days constitutes their supreme happiness.'

Faujas St-Fond was not alone in failing to draw any particular inference from such bleak comparisons, though William Hutton, pausing at Sheffield on his way to Scarborough, noted something very like cause and effect. 'The buildings and the inhabitants are tinged with smoak; the latter look sickly; and themselves assured me that life was of shorter duration than in other places. The Duke of Norfolk, however, has reason to be pleased with it; for report informed me that he draws forty thousand a year, as Lord of the place.'

Such examples might appear extreme, but we can get no sort of perspective on the tourists' attitudes unless their relative position is known – 'poor' has no meaning unless we also know what we mean by 'rich'. It was not just a question of cash in the pocket, but of a wholly different way of life. Faujas St-Fond described the activities of a typical day at Inverary Castle.

We remained three whole days in this delightful retreat, devoting the mornings to natural history and the evenings to music and conversation . . . The manner in which we spent our time at Inverary castle was extremely agreeable. Each person rose at any hour he pleased in the morning. Some took a ride, others went to the chace. I rose with the sun and proceeded to examine the natural history of the environs . . . At ten o'clock a bell summoned us to breakfast: we then repaired to a large room. Here we found several breakfast tables, covered with tea, coffee, excellent cream, and everything the appetite could desire, surrounded with bouquets of flowers, newspapers and books. There were, besides, in this room, a billiard-table, a piano-forte, and other musical instruments.

After breakfast, some walked in the parks, others amused themselves with reading and music, or returned to their apartments . . . At half past four, the dinner bell was rung, and we went to the dining room, where we always found a table of twenty-five or thirty covers.

Staying in a country house was scarcely a strenuous experience, but even at the more modest level of accommodation the life of the tourist could not be described as hard. The Rev. Warner reported on a supper in a Welsh inn consisting of sole, trout, mutton steaks, vegetable, bread and cheese and three tankards of porter plus bed and breakfast – and all for the sum of five shillings and twopence. It sounds good value, cheap at the price – cheap that is until you measure it against the wages paid to working men and their families. Take, for example, the pay of stocking manufacturers at Kendal on the fringe of the tourists' beloved Lake District. The combers were highest paid by far at ten shillings and sixpence a week, and after that the rates dropped to spinners at three shillings, knitters at two shillings and sixpence and children at two shillings. But for the most telling comparison between the wages of the Kendal stockingers and the costs of the Lakeland tourists, one should look back at the coach fares quoted earlier. To the London traveller who stopped off to look at the knitters at work, the cost of the round trip would have been just over one year's wages.

So, if we look at the poor through the eyes of the rich tourist, what do we see? Often, of course, very little. The homes of the poorest of the Scottish poor scarcely disturbed the landscape. 'The houses of the common people,' wrote Thomas Pennant on his visit to the Highlands, 'are shocking to humanity, formed of loose stones, and covered with clods, which they call *devish*, or with heath, broom or branches of fir: they look, at a distance, like so many black mole hills. The inhabitants live very poorly on oatmeal, barley-cakes, and potatoes; they drink whiskey mixed with honey.' But what really made the poor inconspicuous was their very ubiquity. What is always with us does tend to go unnoticed unless forced on to our attention. Prince Pückler-Muskau found that the poor of Snowdonia insisted on being noticed.

> A minor 'tormento' in this region is the multitude of children, who start up and vanish again like gnomes; they pursue the carriage, begging with inconceivable pertinacity. Wearied by their importunity, I had made a positive determination not to give anything to anybody; a single deviation from which rule insures your never being rid of them for a moment. However, one little girl vanquished all my resolutions by her perseverence: she ran at least a German mile [4½ miles] up hill and down dale, at a brisk trot, sometimes gaining upon me a little by a foot-path, but never losing sight of me for a minute. She ran by the side of the carriage, uttering the same ceaseless plaintive wail, like the cry of the sea-mew, which at length became so intolerable to me that I surrendered, and purchased my deliverance from my untireable pursuer at the price of a shilling.

The Prince, even when not being pursued by howling beggars, was much given to philosophising about the society which so neatly provided one way of life for himself and a rather different style for his inferiors. As a good Christian, he may sometimes have found difficulty in reconciling the rules of behaviour that he habitually followed with those recommended in the Scriptures, but never found the task impossible. So we find him, soon after his meeting with the beggar girl, musing over that

puzzling injunction to 'turn the other cheek'. That was
not at all the sort of thing a prince would expect to do.
'Does not the honour of our rank, and of our uniform,
command us instantly and without hesitation, to strike
again a man who should dare to lay hands upon us?'
Then the happy solution to the problem suddenly came to
him. 'Our Saviour intended these words to be taken with
one limitation, – that is, *for the common people*, in whom
it is unquestionably meritorious when struck on one
cheek, instead of giving way to wrath and bitterness, to
offer the other.' So he rode on, satisfied. In general, the
good Prince was inclined to view poverty as a kind of
self-inflicted injury. 'It was, however, just harvest-time,
and the want of labourers in the field so great, that the
farmers gave almost any wages. Nevertheless, I was
assured that the mechanics would rather destroy all the
machinery and actually starve, than take a sickle in their
hands, or bind a sheaf: so intractable and obstinate are
the English common people rendered by their universal
comfort, and the certainty of obtaining employment if
they vigorously seek it.'

That last comment is quite unusual, for it was rare for
tourists to take much note of farm workers. What really
attracted their attention was the new class of industrial
worker. 'Industrial' workers had, in fact, been around for
a very long time, but they had been the old hand workers
of the domestic industry. The wife spinning at her
cottage door could be fitted into the popular idea of a
pastoral scene. It could even seem quite idyllic, as Mrs
Morgan noted when her travels took her through Buckinghamshire.

'It appeared very extraordinary to me, instead of
spinning wheels at every cottage door, as there are
in Essex, Suffolk & Cambridgeshire to see the women
sitting with their lace cushions. I could almost have
persuaded myself there were no poor people in that
country. Making lace seemed such a ladylike employment. I had annexed an idea of its giving peculiar

grace to the motion of a handsome hand and arm, and an additional elegance to slender fingers, when moving betwixt bobbins. I never before saw anybody make lace, but merely for amusement.'

The new industries transformed these scenes of happy domesticity – happy, that is, as described by travellers who did not enquire too closely into the conditions that lay behind them. There were many who were quick to deplore the passing of the old ways which, however flawed, represented stability and order. John Byng was among the most vociferous denouncers of change. He was the complete conservative, and disliked the new towns and the new way of life every bit as much as he disliked the new mill set by a once peaceful river.

My opinion hold, that the labourer has quitted the country; and that Enclosing Acts have in a great measure been the cause. But I shall be answer'd by 'Think you not that our population is as great as formerly?' Why, aye, in many countries where manufactures flourish, I think it is, but they have sucked up the villages and single cottages; Birmingham, Manchester and Sheffield, swarm with inhabitants; but look at them, what a set of mean, drunken wretches! Are they of the make, of honesty, or the use of the husbandmen?

The husbandman works regularly, is sober and industrious, and poorly paid, but the artisan will work (for high wages) but 4 days in a week, and wallow in drink the other 3, and if unemployed, will be ripe for, and active in any mischief. Then in gallop the dragoons, and ride over them!

I dread trade, I hate its clamour: as a gentleman born, I scowl at their advantages. It is in trading towns, only, where rioting and discords begin: and yet they want representatives; why of all places they are the last that should be represented; for their members will be most falsely, and violently chosen and their towns for ever convulsed by faction . . .

Old Sarum is a better, and honester representation, than any great manufacturing town could produce.

There is some support for Byng's views on the venality of manufacturing towns in the writings of William Bray who commented on Northampton, famous for shoe and stocking making: "The inhabitants are numerous and, unhappily, every freeman, resident or not, and every resident, free or not, has a vote in the election of M.P.s for the town; their numbers and their infamous venality in 1768, will be long remembered, and severely felt by some noble families in the neighbourhood.'

But, to return to the tourists and the poor, what we almost invariably come back to is the same old concept of the undeserving poor. As a class, the tourists were remarkably keen on combining observation with moral diatribe. Arthur Young commented favourably on the miners of Swinton who kept small gardens 'which, from the great foresight and refined politics of their landlord grew into little farms.' But it turned out to be only a short step from that admirable particular to a more lamentable general observation. 'Miners in general, I might almost say universally, are a most tumultuous, sturdy set of people, greatly impatient of control, very insolent and much void of common industry. Those employed in the lead mines of Craven, and in many collieries, can scarcely, by any means, be kept to the performance of a regular business; upon the least disgust, they quit their service and try another. No bribes can tempt them to any industry after the first performance of their stated work, which leaves them half the day for idleness, or rioting at the alehouse.'

Left unsaid is the fact that the miners' work started at midnight; the period when Young would have liked to see them tending their gardens was the time left over after a twelve-hour shift. Apart from the hard work, the lead miners were subjected to an unpleasant disease known as 'ballan', one of the effects of which was constipation which, according to Warner, could last up to two weeks.

The miners might well have argued that even if they hadn't earned their drop of beer, it was an essential medicine.

A French visitor to the Durham coalfield, M. Pichot, reached very different conclusions about the miners, and commented on their good health, which he attributed to the fact that 'they are preserved from the vicissitudes of the weather'. Descending several hundred feet to a hot, dirty unventilated coal mine seems a strange way of getting in out of the rain.

There was a general feeling among the tourists, who were, after all, as representative a sample of the gentry as one could expect to find, that the poor should be kept as busy as possible for as long as possible. Nevertheless, the tourists were often genuinely horrified at the conditions of the workers in the new factories. J. Grant, taking the popular tour of Derbyshire and the Lakes, stopped off to see the dinner-time exodus from a cotton mill. He noted the pale faces of the workers, the cotton particles stuck to their clothes, and was ready to deplore the conditions which made them breathe an atmosphere thick with the cotton dust that brought on lung disease. He offered his own remedy to mill owners.

> Let every such person, then, order his work-people to bathe every morning, and let them have a piece of play-ground for them, wherein some athletic and innocent exercise might be enjoyed for an hour or two, each day. In cotton-works, let each of them drink much water; and to crown the whole establish a Sunday school, where they might be instructed orally, without being taught to read.

Why no reading? Because if all the teaching was oral, then the pupils would only learn what the teachers wanted them to know. But how, the manufacturers might have asked, was all this going to help them? Mr Grant was ready with his answer.

> Enter into a resolution not to give the present

exorbitant wages of 2s to the meanest hand, and yet keep them so far above the wages of agriculture, as to excite temptation. Where 18d is the day's receipt of a labourer, 2d makes a wonderful odds. At present how does the matter stand? Why thus; the manufacture gets 4s in two days, and this enables him to ruin his health by drunkenness, and his mind by idleness on the third.

His money spent and his mind enfeebled, he returns unwillingly again to work, discontented, and cursing all laws, human and divine, which have so arranged matters that yon stately house, and the gilded coach in which its owner rides, should belong to what the Corresponding Society, the illuminati and illuminates of this country, have deluded him into the idea, is an individual, with no better claim to it than himself.

Remember the cost of the three-week tour? Now look again at the 'exorbitant' wages. But it is not enough to throw up one's hands in horror as tourist after tourist makes similar comments. One has to keep in mind that they were only accepting the ethic of the day: to provide the poor with work was an inestimable blessing, preserving them from unimaginable evils. The old saw, 'the devil finds work for idle hands,' was taken as having a quite literal meaning. So Hutton, seeing a group of debtors in York, could comment with great piety: 'The lower classes cannot be taught a better lesson than the habit of industry. When a man has only his *hands* to depend on, guide those hands into employment. This will enable him to live respected, supply him with necessaries for existence, prevent temptations to pilfer and lessen the use of the prison and the gallows.' It will not perhaps have escaped notice that these moral physicians did not propose similar treatment for themselves.

The same basic attitudes account for the acceptance of what, to modern eyes, seems the most repugnant aspect of the industrial revolution – the use and abuse of child workers. We are so used to thinking of this as an evil that it comes as something of a shock to find the tourists regarding it as a blessing. The Duke of Rutland visited the Swansea pottery and noted with pleasure: 'This work indeed employs a part of those people who otherwise would remain idle and unemployed; namely women and children of either sex.' But his delight was mild compared with the rapture with which W. Hutchinson viewed the carpet makers of Penrith. 'The spinning of this work is done by children from the foundling Hospital. Tears of pleasure gushed upon the eye, to behold those poor orphans, who would otherwise perhaps have been totally lost to the world and to themselves, thus, by so excellent a charity, saved from the hands of destruction and vice, rendered useful members of society, and happy in their industry and innocence.' And Thomas Pennant took up the theme at the Whitehaven workhouse: 'With pleasure I observed old age, idiocy, and even infants of three years of age, contributing to their own support, by the pulling of oakum.' Where the tourists wept for pleasure, we see only pain.

A different approach to the poor was on view at New Lanark – a popular stopping-off place which boasted a large cotton factory and had the splendidly picturesque Clyde falls nearby as a bonus. The Duke of Rutland went there and greatly approved what he saw of David Dale and his works. 'We were struck by the excellence of his arrangements with regard to the health, order, and morals of his work-people, in which his benevolence, no less than his good sense, was obvious. His plan must indeed be considered a model, and it furnishes a convincing proof that most of the objections to manufactures on the score of their injurious influence on the persons employed in them, may be obviated by management and attention.' He was equally pleased to hear that although the pernicious *Rights of Man* by Tom Paine had circulated among the work people, Dale had been quick to retaliate with the Bishop of Llandaff's *Apology for the Bible* and 'had soon the satisfaction of finding them convinced by it, and restored to their quiet settled habits of thinking and acting.' Reassured about the physical and moral welfare of the inhabitants of New Lanark, the duke could relax and enjoy himself, by visiting the falls by moonlight.

By the time Robert Southey visited New Lanark in 1819, the works were under the control of the man who was to make the name famous – Robert Owen. Instead of being taken to see the children at work, he was treated to a dancing display, if treated is the right word.

> Half a dozen fine boys, about nine or ten years old, led the way, playing on fifes, and some 200 children, from four years of age till ten, entered the room and arranged themselves on three sides of it. A man whose official situation I did not comprehend gave the word, which either because of the tone or the dialect I did not understand; and they turned to the right or left, faced about, fell forwards and backwards, and stamped at command, performing manoeuvres the object of which was not very clear, with perfect regularity . . . I could not but think that these puppet-like motions might, with a little ingenuity, have been produced by the great waterwheel.

He concluded, not surprisingly, that 'there was too much of all this', though he was honest enough to add that 'the children seemed to like it'. Southey may not have been impressed by the dancing, but he was enchanted with the very youngest children. One of the features of New Lanark was the area set aside for them to play, under supervision – a kind of early play group. 'They made a glorious noise, worth all the concerts of New Lanark, and of London to boot. It was really delightful to see how the little creatures crowded about Owen to make their bows and their curtsies, looking up and smiling in his face; the genuine benignity and pleasure with which he noticed them.' Here was something healthier than shedding tears of delight over the sight of a three year old working full time. Southey was a far from blinkered observer. He commented on the cleanliness of the streets which he admitted were better than most Scots towns, but still grumbled that they were 'not quite so clean as they ought to be', and while approving of the Company stores, took good care to satisfy himself that the people 'may deal elsewhere if they chuse'. New Lanark represented one end of the industrial scale, the work-house paupers the other.

The attitudes of the tourists towards the poor may have been coloured by the general attitudes of the age in which they lived, but the insight the accounts give us into those attitudes is perhaps less important than the fact of their troubling to observe and record so many details of their alien life. They are important because the poor were in no position to make records of their own and any view, however biased, is better than none at all. Often the tourists took a good deal of trouble to collect such information. For example, the tourists who went to Parys mountain to enthuse over a particularly devastating form of open cast mining, often went on to see Amlwch, the tiny village which had been overwhelmed by the huge influx of miners. In the 1760s, Amlwch had a population of around two hundred, but by the time Arthur Aikin went there in 1797 it had grown to some four to five thousand. From his account we learn that there were 1200 miners and 90 smelters, that pay varied between a shilling and twenty pence a day, and that they produced 20–40,000 tons of copper a year. As well as giving these statistics, Aikin also provides a fascinating glimpse into the way of life of the place. He went on to see the miners at their rest time and found, to his considerable surprise, that the men were sitting peaceably listening, while one of them read aloud the whole of that day's newspaper. The children were being organised into races. 'To one who had been a spectator of the gross and riotous delight too frequent on holiday evenings in the outskirts of the metropolis, or any large town in England, the contrast could not fail of being very striking, and much to the advantage of the inhabitants of Amlwch: out of the whole number we did not see one drinking party; the pleasures of Society and mutual converse needed not the aid of intoxication to heighten their relish.'

Drunkenness, disorder and unmentionable evils were what the tourist expected to find among the poor, so that the absence of those characteristics always seemed to merit comment. Robert Heron, for instance, toured western Scotland in 1792 and looked in on the extensive lead mines at Leadhills and Wanlockhead. The two villages are set in moorland country on the Dumfries-Lanark border – 'bleak, wild and lofty'. Here he found a desperately hard-worked population. 'The labour of the miners is severe and unremitting. Through night and day, it is continued; one class relieving another, by turns of eight hours each.' On top of this, because of the remoteness of the region, 'these villagers have naturally been obliged to form little kitchen-gardens, and to cover small patches of the adjacent ground with corn and potatoes. Every tender vegetable has here, indeed, a dwarfish, stunted aspect.' Yet, in spite of all this hard work, 'These miners find time for reading. They have even furnished themselves with a common library which contains a considerable number of good English authors. Many of them are of the religious sect of the Seceders or of the McMillanites [two non-conformist sects that had broken away from the Church of Scotland].' Here, one would have thought, was a community that deserved praise, meeting every requirement in good measure – industrious, both at work and play, studious, sober and religious too. But do they get such praise? They do not. For it appears to Mr Heron that the cause of this almost excessive virtue lay with the wise proprietors who kept their employees too poor to find time or energy for sin. The system in the villages – which Mr Heron most seriously recommended to all employers – consisted of providing the workers with oatmeal 'at a certain price' (unspecified) which was deducted from their pay. The rest of the wages was paid in cash in arrears – not weekly, not even monthly, but by the quarter or even the half year. Heron did not, however, mention another aspect of the work of the area. Thomas

Pennant did. He visited Leadhills where 'neither tree nor shrub, nor verdure, nor picturesque rock, appear to amuse the eye'. He gave an account of 'lead distemper' or 'mill reak' which 'brings on palsies, and sometimes madness, terminating in death in about ten days'.

Miners seemed to come in for a good deal of attention one way or another, and, as with other groups, one longs to know what they in their turn thought of the gentry. The Welsh miners visited by Mrs Morgan must have been startled by the sudden appearance of such a very grand lady, uninvited, among them, though she herself seemed to regard her activities as perfectly normal.

> Though I had not the courage to descend a coal-pit, I ventured to crawl into a miner's hut, for you cannot enter any other way than on your hands and knees: when in, you can only just stand upright near the middle of it where there is a large fire of this country coals, which are very different from ours. They emit a steam that is intolerable in a close place, such as I am now describing, where there is only an aperture in the top by way of chimney. Though they eat in these huts, yet I saw no culinary utensils nor household furniture, not even a bench of turf round the hovel to sit down upon. The miners sit upon their hams, as the Indians do. In Byron's voyage, there is a print of what he calls a whigwham or Indian hut, which will give you a perfect idea of these habitations; and the people, except that they are clothed, bear a strong resemblance to the natives of Terra del Fuego. You are to observe that these are only temporary erections, where they eat, and take rest at intervals from their labour, or shelter from a storm. They have all cottages in the village.

Mrs Morgan, like many of her contemporaries, was just plain old-fashioned nosey and we, of a later generation, have good reason to be grateful to the tourists' insatiable curiosity. Without their comments, our knowledge of that age, especially our knowledge of the lives of ordinary

Arthur Young, agriculturalist and traveller, was one of many tourists fascinated by Britain's industrial revolution. His sketch *below* shows a boat passing over one of the smaller aqueducts on the Bridgewater Canal.

Parys Mountain in Anglesey was quarried and mined
for copper. It had, in consequence, 'a most savage
appearance.'

The famous Darby ironworks at Coalbrookdale. In the
foreground a team of horses pulls a steam-engine
cylinder past the furnaces.

The throwing room at
Josiah Wedgwood's
Etruria works.

Industrial picturesque: a forge near Dolgellau.

Some travellers took notes about the
people they met along the way;
Rowlandson, who toured with Henry
Wigstead, drew them. *left* A Welsh
landlady; *below* A kitchen in Newcastle.
The dog in the treadmill is keeping
the roast turning by the fire.

men and women, would be that much the poorer. On the vexed question of living standards, for example, there are countless snippets of information to be gathered. Arthur Young, with his special interest in agriculture, toured with the specific aim of collecting data, and his books are full of statistics that are of special value to the professional historian. At the same time he was given to making more general observations that were very much the tourist's stock in trade. So, in Manchester, after detailing wage rates and numbers employed, he came up with this observation about the attitudes of the inhabitants. 'In general, all the branches find, that their best friend is an high price of provisions . . . The master manufacturers of Manchester wish that prices might always be high enough to enforce a general industry; to keep the hands employed six days for a week's work.' He claimed, not surprisingly, that he had his information from an employer, but when he added that the work people also preferred this arrangement as it kept them from drunkenness, the reader may be excused a little mild scepticism.

The tourists found all manner of things about the poor to be of interest. They took notes on such matters as health, or the lack of it, and what was being done about it. Arthur Young contributed this alarming account of the work of the Sheffield grinders: 'The grindstones turn with such amazing velocity, that by the mere force of motion they now and then fly in pieces, and kill the men at work on them . . . of late years they have invented a method of chaining down an iron over the stone on which the men work in such a manner, that in the case of the above mentioned accidents, the pieces of stone can only fly forwards; and not upwards; and yet men by the force of the breaking have been thrown back in a surprising manner, and their hands struck off by shivers of the stone.' Injury and illness were serious matters, and Hutchinson noted the way in which the people of Barnard's Castle attempted to solve their own problems.

In this place the manufacturers (of woollen goods)

have established societies or clubs, in which they contribute monthly towards making a fund for the relief of their members, when sick, lame, blind or by old age rendered incapable of following business. These institutions afford a comfortable assistance to a great number of people, there being no less than nine of these associations here, consisting of near one hundred each, every indigent member receiving three shillings and sixpence weekly and upon death, five pounds are paid to the representative of the deceased, towards his funeral etc. These excellent institutions are but little encouraged by the land-owners, although the poor rate is thereby greatly exonerated.

The most humane view of the sick was taken by William Mavor, when he came to consider that great scourge of the age, smallpox.

What cause there is for regret that vaccination is not recommended by every public and private authority, and that the children of the poor do not receive it gratuitously! One person properly qualified would be sufficient to attend a whole county; and if he had a moderate salary allowed him for vaccinating the poor, with what the rich would gladly pay, he might derive a comfortable subsistence from his labour. The resident surgeons and apothecaries are generally hostile to the practice because it cuts off a beneficial branch of the trade.

There is something familiar about the arguments surrounding this particular proposal which could well have been quoted with approval by the modern architect of the National Health Service. But how would Bevan have reacted to this statement by the same author in the same book? The poor 'care not how much they abuse, or rob or injure their superiors provided they can do it with impunity.' That is the same author and, indeed, the same book.

One thing the tourists were always on the look out for

was the whimsical or strange, and they occasionally found it more by accident than by intent. Methodism was just beginning to take a hold among the Welsh poor in the eighteenth century and the Duke of Rutland had the opportunity to see something of it at first hand, when he visited Swansea. 'This morning at eleven o'clock we intended to go to church. Instead we got into a Methodist meeting-house, where a set of fellows were assembled round a preacher, from whose lips issued forth the most unintelligible jargon of nonsense I ever heard. Our mistake was curious, but could not be rectified, and we were forced to sit till it was over, which was not till near one o'clock.' Sometimes the oddity was as much in the tourist's mind as in what he described. There is, for example, nothing especially odd about allotments, but George Lipscomb made them seem strange by the curious condescension he showed in describing these perfectly ordinary patches of land, worked, as far as one can tell, in a perfectly ordinary way by the inhabitants of Birmingham.

> Almost every housekeeper is possessed of a little spot of land near the town, though perhaps at some distance from his habitation; and thither he retires every evening in the summer season, as soon as the fatigues of business are over to breathe a purer air, and innocently employ himself in cultivating his cabbages & pot-herbs. The appearance of these minute enclosures is whimsical, and the ornament of a small summerhouse or alcove, in which the proprietor frequently enjoys the *sublime* amusement of *smoking* is indeed a very graceful addition to the picture: but the wholesomeness and advantage to which the cultivation of these slips of industry has a direct tendency, makes the friend of social happiness overlook their defects.

These attitudes are perfectly illustrated in the following passage. The writer is Wyndham, the subject the Welsh poor.

The state of the common people in the low lands of

this country, and particularly of the women, to whose lot the most laborious drudgery belong, seems miserable beyond the idea of an Englishman to conceive; a foreigner would scarcely be persuaded, that they lived under the protection of the same laws, or that they enjoyed the same rights and privileges with their English neighbours.

Their habitations are low, mud-built hovels, raised over the natural earth, which is as deficient in point of level within as without. Notwithstanding the severity of the climate, the windows are frequently destitute of a single piece of glazing. If the inhabitants wish to enjoy the light, they must at the same time suffer the cold: they wear neither shoes nor stockings, and chiefly subsist upon the coarse diet of rank cheese, oat bread, and milk. Such penury anticipates old age, and I have seen persons of forty, from their decrepid and wrinkled features, appear, as if they had passed their grand climacteric. A melancholy dejection is spread over their countenances, which are strangers to the smiles of cheerfulness and pleasure.

If we carry our observations to the mountains, we shall find, among those dreary wastes, a poverty still more extreme than below; in many of those parishes a grain of wheat has never been seen; even the cheap luxury of garden greens is unknown; and according to the strong expression of a lowland Welshman, there are hundreds of families, who have never tasted a leek. They continue in the same unimproved state, as in the time of Giraldus . . . Notwithstanding this apparent misery, we cannot pronounce these mountaineers miserable; if content be happiness, they are certainly happy: They are all equally poor, and while poverty is not particular, it cannot be considered as a misfortune. They are robust, healthy, and live to a great age, and as they are ignorant of those many refinements, which civilized luxury has taught us to consider as necessaries of life, they have therefore no want of them, there is

The Rich Man in his Castle, the Poor Man at his Gate

'No craving void left aching in their breast.'

For this reason, we see mirth and cheerfulness, united with poverty, in the most humble cot upon the highlands, when a smaller degree of poverty has spread a discontented gloom, over the whole face of the lowlands. All happiness is by comparison, so these lower people are comparatively miserable: for they are tantalized with appetites which they cannot gratify, while they behold with envy, many pleasures enjoyed by others, which partial nature has forbidden them even to hope for.

6

Travellers in a Foreign Land

TODAY'S travellers range over Europe and far beyond
in their search for exotica: the Georgian tourist had
no need of such long journeys. The English traveller,
for example, need go no further than Wales to discover
a land as foreign and customs as bizarre as any modern
anthropologist might expect to discover on an expedition
up the Amazon. James Boswell made the same point to
his travelling companion in Scotland:

> At Auchnasheal, we sat down on a green turf-seat at
> the end of a house; they brought us out two wooden
> dishes of milk, which we tested. One of them was
> frothed like a syllabub. I saw a woman preparing it
> with a stick as is used for chocolate, and in the same
> manner. We had a considerable circle about us, men,
> woman and children, all McCraes, Lord Seaforth's
> people. I observed to Dr Johnson, it was much the
> same as being with a tribe of Indians. – JOHNSON.
> 'Yes, sir: but not so terrifying.'

And there you have the nub of it: all the excitement and
thrills of foreign travel, but with fewer dangers and
inconveniences.

Scotland was perhaps the most exotic of all the home
countries. Here tourists could find places unvisited by
other travellers, where the locals spoke a foreign tongue
and indulged in all manner of curious customs. Such odd-
ness was not always to the liking of the well-bred English
traveller, as Henry Skrine noted on his first encounter
with the Scots. As he reached Gretna Green, he was

astonished to see an abrupt change from the conditions in
England.

> My eyes encountered, in a cluster of mud-built sheds,
> a number of miserable wretches, ragged, bare-footed
> and squalid, almost beyond the power of description.
> Nor was this misery confined to a single spot: for it
> attended every village, and almost every countenance
> I met with, in my way to Glasgow. Such wretched-
> ness is naturally the offspring of idleness, ignorance
> and necessity . . . this deplorable state of the common
> people greatly discredits a country to which nature
> has been in other respects very munificent.

Even in the eighteenth century Gretna Green was
famous as the spot where runaways could come to be
married over the anvil; though when the Duke of Rutland
called in for a chat, he found the blacksmith to be blind
drunk! But to return to Skrine and his jaundiced view of
the Scots: there was not a good word on the nation to be
had from him.

> It must be confessed, however, that the common
> people of Scotland are more than a century behind
> the English in improvement; and the manners of the
> lowlanders in particular cannot fail to disgust a
> stranger. All the stories that are propagated of the
> filth & habitual dirtiness of this people are surpassed
> by the reality; and the squalid unwholesome appear-
> ance of their garb and countenances, is exceeded by
> the wretchedness that prevails within their houses.
> Their manners are equally unpleasant being un-
> communicative and forbidding in the extreme; and
> whole groups of villagers fly from the approach of a
> traveller, like the most untamed of savages.

Many tourists took a similarly uncharitable view of the
northern Britons: even Boswell regarded many of his
fellow countrymen with contempt. Dr Johnson had a
Highland guide for part of their journey, who had heard
him express pleasure at the sight of some browsing goats.

As the doctor was having one of his periodic grumbles, this youth decided to try to restore him to a better humour, much to Boswell's amusement. 'The fellow cried, with a very Highland accent "See such pretty goats!" Then he whistled *whu!* and made them jump. – Little did he conceive what Dr Johnson was. Here now was a common ignorant Highland clown imagining that he could divert, as one does a child – Dr Samuel Johnson! – The ludicrousness, absurdity, and extraordinary contrast between what the fellow fancied, and the reality, was truly comick.'

There were many complaints about Highland uncouthness, but few could fault the genuine good feeling towards strangers that lay behind Scots hospitality. It might not have been the sort of hospitality that the travellers were used to enjoying in the houses of their friends, but it was the more remarkable in being freely offered by those who had so little. When the French geologist Faujas St-Fond landed on Staffa, 'the men, women and children, first formed themselves in a large circle around us and our seamen. Then one of the women, whose appearance was rendered most disgusting by filth and ugliness brought out a large wooden bowl filled with milk, with which she placed herself in the center of the circle. She served us all round with attention and immediately came up to me, and pronouncing some words, presented the bowl with a sort of courtesy. I held out my hands to receive it; but she drank some of it before she gave it to me. I followed the example, and passed the vessel to William Thornton, who was next to me; he gave it to Mr McDonald; and it was thus passed from hand to hand, or more properly, from mouth to mouth till every person had tasted of it.'

Not that everything St-Fond received in the Hebrides was equally welcome. At Iona, he managed to get himself infested with lice. He also discovered that among such a hospitable people, the acceptance of hospitality can have great social significance. He was entertained right royally at Dalmally by the local blacksmith, MacNab, who gave his visitors a formal drink from a bowl of milk, followed by butter cakes and whiskey. When they left, they were at once invited for further refreshments by a neighbour 'who was richer and more ostentatious than MacNab' and who had dressed his wife up in 'her best finery' for the occasion. The visitors politely declined, pleading pressure of time, and went on their way. A Scots friend explained to them the enormity of this breach of etiquette. 'You have painfully wounded the feelings of that family, who are in easy circumstances, and much respected in the country, by refusing to enter their habitations while you visited that of MacNab. That sort of exclusive preference is regarded as very humiliating among the Highlanders.' They returned to the house, but the door was closed in their faces.

Generosity and poverty may have been the most striking characteristics of the people, but what really fascinated the visitors were the strange customs which made life so different from that of their native England. Thomas Pennant made notes of a number of these customs. 'A Highlander never begins anything of consequence on the day of the week on which the 3rd May falls, which he styles nagh Sheachanna na bleanagh or the dismal day.' Or again: 'Before women bake their bannocks or oatmeal cakes they make a cross on the last.' And a custom which, though relating to babies, clearly had an effect on the adults too: 'Midwives give new-born babes a small spoonful of earth and whiskey as the first food they take.' The English observers of these different customs took precisely the view that has characterised the English tourist ever since: anything that is not just as it is at home must be comical. Mary Ann Hanway who visited the Highlands in the 1770s clearly found the sight of the foreign Scots going to church, highly entertaining.

I was last Sunday, for the first time, at a Highland Kirk, or church; and such a strange appearance as the lower sort of women make would amaze you. The married ones wear a handkerchief crossed over their heads, with two ends pinned under their chin, and the third flying behind; the young ones wear nothing

but a ribband on their hair; the other parts of their
dress are like those of the common people with us;
only over all, they wear a plaid, which reaches to
their feet, and is wrapped over their head, so that
nothing is left to be seen but their noses. The poorest
sort of all, who cannot afford a plaid, rather than not
be ornamented, walk forth arrayed in their blankets;
so that when all are assembled in this strange fashion
they really have just the appearance of a set of
lunaticks.

She took a similarly uncomprehending view of another
Scots speciality – the bagpipe. 'In many houses, they
still retain the ancient custom of the piper playing all
the time the company are at dinner, on his *horrid bagpipes*;
this is to me more dreadful than the grunting of pigs, the
screaming of owls and the squalling of cats. All these
creatures in a concert would be to my ears pleasing,
compared to that discordant instrument to which I have
a natural antipathy.' In the end she was able to pay the
Scots one compliment – she found Scotland, unlike
England, to be quite free of highwaymen.

One popular tourist pastime was jotting down notes
about the local women. There were few comments on
how the local men dressed, even fewer on whether they
were handsome or plain: but there were full descriptions
of what women wore, and the tourists seem to have been
running their own kind of early 'Miss Britain' contest,
judging by the numbers of comments on the beauty or
otherwise of the local females. They liked to make sweep-
ing generalisations. Thomas Pennant was quite ready
to condemn the whole of Scots womanhood as plain, but
at least he cannot be accused of male chauvinism, for he
was equally hard on the men.

The men are thin, but strong; idle and lazy, except
employed in the chace or anything that looks like
amusement; are content with their hard fare, and will
not exert themselves farther than to get what they
deem necessaries. The women are more industrious,

spin their own husbands cloaths, and get money by knitting stockings, the great trade of the country. The common women are in general most remarkably plain, and soon acquire an old look, and by being much exposed to the weather without hats, such a grin, and contraction of the muscles, as heightens greatly their natural hardness of features: I never saw so much plainness among the lower ranks of females: but the *ne plus ultra* of hard features is not found till you arrive among the fish-women at Aberdeen.

Mrs Hanway seemed, at first, to be equally down on the ladies. She visited Edinburgh where she noted that what 'most shocks English delicacy is, to see all the streets filled with the lower class of women, that wear neither shoes nor stockings.' It appears that quite the most shocking aspect of this state of affairs was that the women in question dressed in that way as much from choice as from necessity. 'I actually heard a young Highland woman say she thought the greatest punishment that could be inflicted on her was the being obliged to wear shoes; but though she was now tolerably reconciled to them, she never could prevail on herself to bear the confinement of stays.' Our sympathies are with the Highland girl. But whatever the shortcomings of the lower orders, Mrs Hanway was able to declare the ladies of Edinburgh 'the great *sublime in beauty*' – mostly, it seems, on the basis of their size being 'five feet eight, or even nine'. So, in the beauty stakes, the Scots at least enjoyed an advantage of height. But the greatest champion of Scots, or at any rate Glasgow, women, turns out to be the Frenchman Faujas St-Fond.

I was astonished, in a climate so cold and so humid as that of Glasgow, to see the greater part of the lower class of females, and even many of those in easy circumstances, walking about with their heads and their feet bare, their bodies covered only with a jump and a gown and petticoat of red stuff, which descended to the middle of their legs: and their fine long hair hanging down without any other ornament than a crooked comb to keep back that part which would otherwise fall over their faces. As there is nothing to fetter their movements, they display an elegance and agility in their part so much the more striking as they are in general tall, well made and of a charming figure. They have a clear complexion and very white teeth. It is not to be inferred, because they walk barefoot, that they are neglectful of cleanliness; for it appears that they wash frequently, and with equal facility both their feet & their hands. In a word, the women of Glasgow will be always seen with pleasure by the lovers of simple nature.

As more travellers visited Wales than Scotland, there are more accounts of Welsh life and customs and, consequently, more comments on Welsh women. William Mavor praised their hard work. Visiting Brecknock, he found that the women 'have every appearance of being industrious; they knit while they are walking and spin while they are nursing.' He also mentioned the feature of early ageing which Pennant had noted among the Scots – an inevitable by-product of overwork and poverty. 'Since we left Gloucester we have seen few handsome faces; the females early become haggard; and though generally well formed, they are seldom striking. Their eyes are their best feature. We observed several mothers with children in their arms who would have passed for granddams in England.' But then, as E. D. Clarke pointed out, the women worked at least as hard as the men, and often at the same jobs. 'Labour seems equally divided between men and women, and it is as common to meet a female driving the plough as it is to see Taffy seated at the milk pail.' Dress and customs of the Welsh seemed, to the English tourists, to be every bit as strange as those of the Scots.

Here [Trecastle] we witnessed a Welsh washing by the side of the stream. A kettle placed on two stones

was kept boiling by a fire of sticks, and one woman
was attending to this department. Another was
stamping with her naked feet in a large tub, filled
with clothes; and a third was beating the linen on a
wooden horse with a beetle, and occasionally rinsing
it in the running stream. As we approached, they
were singing very merrily, but they ceased on seeing
us; and when they perceived that one of the party was
taking them off or in other words making a sketch of
the scene, it was with some difficulty we could get
them to resume their occupations. The only dress they
wore, was a striped flannel petticoat, a shift, and a
black beaver hat.

The author of these words, Mrs Morgan, was equally
surprised by the appearance of the Welsh women. She
made these comments on the 'little farmers' wives' who
came to Llandovery fair to sell their corn. 'There being
a fair held today, my surprize is very great, instead of
seeing peasants walking barefoot, dirty and poorly clad,
to find a hundred or two of women all on horseback and
most of them in a uniform dress, which is a blue cloth
jacket and petticoat, and black beaver hat. The neatness
and decency of this is a striking contrast to the gay and
tawdry cottons worn by English women of this order.'
But her astonishment was as nothing compared to that
of the Rev. J. Evans who was shaved by a female barber
who, he was forced to admit, did the job rather well. He
also noted the preference for going barefoot. The women
would carry their shoes to church, wash their feet in a
stream and then, decently shod, enter the building.

From women in general to two women in particular:
the famous Ladies of Llangollen. Most writers found
some difficulty in describing this interesting phenomenon
of two ladies who left homes and families so that they
could live together, without giving offence. The Rev.
Evans carried it off quite neatly.

At a small distance, overlooking the town, is a very
neat building in the cottage style, fitted up with

great taste by the present occupiers, the Right Hon.
Lady Eleanor Butler and Miss Ponsonby. The former
was sister to John, late Earl of Ormond, and is aunt
of the present Earl . . . These ladies, united by sisterly
affection, congenial talents, and endued with virtues
and accomplishments, calculated to adorn more
public scenes, retired early from the gay world, and
chose this recluse spot for their constant residence.
Avoiding every appearance of dissipation they lead
a life as retired as the situation.

The activities of these two ladies aroused considerable
interest, mainly because of their high social standing, but
the sex life of the ordinary people of Wales was scarcely
less fascinating to the tourists. The main feature that
variously interested and appalled the tourists was the
practice of 'bundling' as described here by William
Mavor.

In regard to the Welsh mode of courtship, among
the peasantry, about which so much has been said
pro and *con* in the counties of Cardigan, Caernarvon
and Merioneth at least, the following we affirmed to
be a fact. When two young persons have agreed to
visit each other, the woman soon receives her admirer
into her chamber, and they court sitting or lying on
her bed. The natural consequence is, that the female
becomes pregnant; and it is seldom that a marriage
takes place without that being the case. To the honour
however of the Welsh gallants, it must be confessed,
that they very rarely desert the woman who has made
them happy; nor does either sex feel any impropriety
in the practice to which we have referred.

There is a sting in the tail of this account, for Mavor
makes it clear that however strange or immoral the
English might consider the Welsh, the Welsh reciprocated
with an even lower view of the English. 'To a stranger,
a Welsh female would be as reserved as any woman on
earth could be. She knows he is not to be trusted.' He

also adds, for good measure, that the wives 'are generally faithful, dutiful and affectionate'. The Rev. Warner noted that the practice had been exported to America, 'which is supposed to have contributed greatly to the *rapid increase in population.*'

In fact, bundling did seem to flourish in those areas where the need to renew the family line or increase the population was particularly strong. This was certainly the case with the scattered rural communities of Wales, and it was even more true of the island of Portland, just off the Dorset coast. Here there was an almost feudal society, and family lineage was all important. 'The Portlanders,' wrote W. G. Maton, 'it seems, have for ages, inter-married only with the natives of their own district but, what is still more remarkable, a man never marries until his intended bride shows signs of pregnancy, and it scarcely ever happens that he proves unfaithful to her or unwilling to marry, because in that case he would be disgraced, and never more acknowledged by his country-men.' Bundling was in fact a practical solution to a practical problem, the need to test fertility.

The most careful observer of the Welsh was probably Mrs Morgan, who gave this valuable advice to her fellow tourists. 'Everything that I have seen since concurs in making me think, if people who travel into a distant part of the kingdom would use the eyes of their own under-standing, instead of taking everything for granted that has been said by former writers, we should not have so many false accounts of countries as we have.' She joined earlier writers in commenting on Welsh women, and although giving them a generally favourable appraisal by declaring them to be 'very pretty', she did add that 'their shape has something of the Dutch roundness and plump-ness in it.' But, she was clearly quite taken with the Welsh men: 'The men are remarkably handsome, and in proportion of their number I think I never saw so many anywhere.' She gave as her overall view that 'the strongest trait in the Welsh disposition is the most unaffected good humour,' a view amply confirmed by William Mavor.

The Welsh, as we found on various occasions, especially among the lower classes, seem ashamed of having it suspected that they set their attentions to sale. They accept with an amiable reluctance, what is offered with delicacy and generosity: and this trait in their character is so delightful that we blushed for the selfishness of our own countrymen, when contrasted with the manners of the peasantry of the principality. In wishing to be civil, the Welsh are perhaps too inquisitive; but if they sometimes ask too many questions, they are never tired of giving answers, when you appear to interest yourself about their welfare, or evince a partiality for their country.

To return to Mrs Morgan: it is always pleasing to find someone who is not so overwhelmed by the strangeness of what they see as to be unable to make rational assessments. Here she is, for instance, on the traditional dress of the Welsh women.

The hereditary dress of the Welsh women is one of the most commodious, comfortable and simple, that I ever saw adopted by any set of people whatever . . . It consists of a garter-blue cloth jacket and petticoat and a black beaver hat. In some districts they wear brown jackets instead of blue; but they are all made in the same form. The petticoat is rather short and hangs round. The jacket is round also, and the flaps are about a quarter of a yard long. Young people wear them shorter, and edge them with binding of different colours, generally pink: this gives them a very smart appearance.

If this traditional costume is the image most frequently associated with Wales, then it is closely followed by Welsh music, especially the Welsh harp. Today, we think of the Welsh harpist as a figure from a distant age, a contemporary of the medieval minstrel. But the Georgian tourists found him very much in evidence in the Wales of their day. Arthur Aikin noted that most of the harpists who entertained at inns or in the street were blind, and

E. D. Clarke described hearing the music 'in its pure state, from a poor blind female harper', at the Talbot Inn, Aberystwyth. 'A prediliction for Welsh music, would alone have disposed me to listen to the harp; but our blind minstrel with her untaught harmony, called forth all our admiration, and attention became the tribute of pity.' Down-to-earth Mrs Morgan made quite sure that her readers got an accurate picture. Harpists there might be, but not, as others had suggested, behind every bush. No, the poor blind harper is firmly pushed aside as yet another figment of the over-romantic imagination. Mrs Morgan's harpist, when she finally caught up with one, far from being the impoverished beggar of legend, was 'sleek and well fed, and though blind, is as happy as Gavefin could have been under the protection of Prince Elphin.' The one point on which all were agreed was that the music itself was a delight, which put the Welsh one up on the Scots, about whose music the tourists were, to say the least, unenthusiastic.

Music and poetry were at their best at the eisteddfod. Pennant visited Caerwys, the town which had the 'particular glory' of being home to the eisteddfod. He proceeded to give a somewhat dubious history of that event.

These Eisteddfods were the British Olympics. Fired at first with generous emulation, our poets crowded into the list, and carried off the prize, contented with the mere honour of victory. At length, when the competitors became numerous, and the country became oppressed with the multitude, new regulations of course took place. The disappointed candidates were no longer suffered to torture the ears of the principality with their wretched compositions. None but bards of merit were suffered to rehearse their pieces; and minstrels of skill to perform. These went through a long probation; judges were appointed to decide on their respective abilities; and degrees suitable were conferred and permissions granted for exercising their talents.

Travellers were often less happy about the Welsh dialect. 'They have a method universally prevalent among them of saying *indeed* and *yes sure* upon every occasion,' wrote Clarke, and Mrs Morgan took a very poor view of the Welsh accent:

> The most striking difference betwixt the Welsh & the English is their dialect, particularly that of the females; and as they are not at all conscious of it I fear they will not soon get rid of it. It consists of a mixture of Welsh and English, with a strong Welsh accent. To me the Welsh language itself sounds a great deal more musical than this jargon. The ladies are so little sensible of this defect, that many of them believe they are not the least tinctured with it, and have asked me very seriously whether I should know them to be natives of Wales by their speech.

This was a period which might, in a sense, be said to have seen the beginnings of Welsh nationalism, and the supercilious attitude of many of the tourists no doubt encouraged it. The eisteddfod, the Welsh bardic gathering, has a history that goes back to at least the fourth century, but after the union with England it became less frequent. In 1771, the Gwyneddigion Society organised the first eisteddfod to be held for nearly a century. It was part of a general revival of interest in the Welsh language, which accompanied the spread of non-conformist religion. The Methodists, who introduced a Welsh language Bible, helped to make the language 'respectable' again. In 1798, the eisteddfod was held at Caerwys, and it was surely no accident that this spot was chosen. Warner found the locals speaking that 'jargon', which Mrs Morgan so disliked, and he also found out why. In the Caerwys schools, English was the compulsory language. Any lapse into Welsh, even if it was only the use of a single Welsh word, was immediately punished. The offender had to stand up while a large piece of lead was strung around his neck, and this weight came to be known locally as the 'Welsh lump'. The restarting of the eisteddfod seems an appropriate response to such measures, and helped to ensure that Wyndham's prophecies on the fate of the Welsh language remained unfulfilled. 'The Welsh language is sensibly declining in every place, where the connection with England is made easy. This has been made sufficiently obvious to me, even without my own knowledge of the principality: and possibly, within a century, a traveller may meet with as much difficulty in his researches after the remains of the Welsh language, as Mr Barrington did in his tour through Cornwall, in pursuit of the Cornish, where he found but one old woman, near 90 years of age, who could speak it, and but two other old women, who could understand it.'

Foreign accents and customs seem always to have been the stock in trade of the humorist. They are certainly so today, and the customs of the Welsh were thought good for a laugh two centuries ago. It seems seldom to have occurred to the humorist that their blend of condescension and mockery might give offence. But one can almost hear the stirrings of an infant Plaid Cymru when one comes across passages like the following from the Rev. Richard Warner.

Every cottager (almost without an exception) keeps his poney and his cow, the one to assist his labours, the other to furnish him with food. Meat, indeed, he seldom tastes, but his diet is not contemptible – oaten cakes, or bread made by a mixture of wheat and rye, hard cheese, potatoes and excellent butter-milk, furnish a meal substantial and wholesome. The last article, however, is generally diluted with water, and when thus prepared, the beverage is emphatically called *glas ddu* or *blue water*. Fortunately for these happy, simple people, the use of spirits is not known amongst them, and the high price, and small measure of the *cwrrw*, effectually prevent them from injuring their health, and ruining their families, by frequently intoxicating themselves even with this national liquor. I had almost forgotten to observe, that the peasant generally adds to his establishment a sow or a hog; which, when fatted, he carries to market, and sells to assist in paying his rent. These are noble animals in Wales, of a large majestick breed, and much more tame and *gentle* in their *manners* than are English pigs. We attributed this, indeed, in a great measure to *education*; for the hog in these highland regions is generally considered as *one* of the *family*; and is very commonly seen reposing comfortably before the cottage fire, with the children of the peasant sporting around him.

The travellers found the rituals surrounding Welsh death as fascinating as the customs of Welsh life. What struck many visitors was the general noisiness, not to say booziness, of the funerals. Wyndham disapproved. 'The dismal solemnity of these weeping countenances soon evaporated, and the sorrows and sense of the company, were quickly drowned in large potations of ale. Such is the general conclusion of a Welsh meeting, whether it begins with mirth or melancholy.' He took a sour view of Welsh drinking habits, giving his opinion that in Wales the women outnumbered the men because the latter drank themselves to death. They were victims of 'a heavy, glutinous ale' which had 'sufficient charms to debauch the senses of almost the whole principality'. Clarke, on the other hand, was amused by the Welsh way with death. 'Women screaming, children crying, men swearing, dogs howling, cats squalling, formed a scene of all others the most unlike a funeral . . . I defy any one to say (of the Welsh) that their bodies are buried in peace.' Prince Pückler-Muskau, in his turn, was shocked when he met the funeral procession of a man killed in the slate quarries. 'The people who escorted it were so smartly dressed and so decorated with flowers, that I took the procession for a wedding.' Warner confirmed the general hubbub of the Welsh funeral, and added the interesting information that at the graveside, relatives and friends put money on the sexton's spade, which was intended to ease the departed soul out of too long a stay in purgatory. Clearly Methodism had not yet got a tight hold on the country in 1798. It was said that some ministers collected as much as ten pounds in this way: there is no information available as to whether the mourners got good value for money. Of all the writers, only Mrs Morgan seems to have had a good word to say on the subject.

> I was walking one day in the environs of Carmarthen, and happening to cast my eyes in at a window that stood open, I saw a pretty young woman, very neatly dressed, leaning over the edge of a small coffin, with her head resting upon her arm. The coffin stood upon a table under the window, and in it was a beautiful female infant, that looked as if it was not dead, but asleep. The mother was indulging her placid grief by admiring it as it lay, and decorating the corpse with the fairest flowers she could select. She was not a little soothed and gratified at my stopping to take notice of the little angel.

Two further quotes help to summarise the tourists' attitude towards Wales, and go some way to explain the birth of Welsh nationalism. The first, from Henry Wigstead, provides a context for the second. In a few words, he gives a clear picture of the appalling poverty of the place. 'The value of money is scarcely known; they pay the rent of their premises in cattle generally which they breed on their land. Flesh is scarce ever tasted by them; and except when visitors leave behind remnants of wine, ale etc., milk is the principal beverage that passes their lips.' Here now is Wyndham. 'It is as difficult to make a nation, so bigotted to opinion as the Welsh is, change the smallest article in their manners, (however beneficial it might be to them) as it would be to force them to abolish their dress, or their language.'

Perhaps the Scots and Welsh would be interested in knowing what the English tourists thought of their own fellow countrymen. Well, they were certainly ready enough to give their views, on the women at least. 'The

137

women of Lancashire,' we are informed by the Rev. William MacRitchie, who should surely have had his mind on something other than ladies' legs, 'seem to be, in general, of an agreeable person, a remarkably good look, and a sound, healthy constitution. They have something *bewitching* about them, indeed: but many of the finest looking country girls wear black stockings on the week-days, which is by no means an improvement to their charms.' The claims of Lancashire received a strong challenge from the Isle of Wight, where J. Hassell made out a case for the local girls. 'When I mention the market I must not forget to notice also the farmers' daughters who resort to it with the produce of their farms, and at once grace it with the charms of their persons, and the winning affability of their behaviour. There is not perhaps in the kingdom a place where so many lovely girls attend the market as at Newport; and at the same time they are dressed with a degree of elegance far beyond what is usually observable in persons of their rank.' The beauty of the female islanders was clearly considered by the local clergymen to constitute a dire threat to the morals of the male islanders. They posted up an abstract from an Act of Parliament passed in the reign of James I which reminded the citizens that 'every female who unfortunately intrudes on the parish a second illegitimate child shall be liable to imprisonment and hard labour in Bridewell for six months.' Hassell had no doubt where his sympathies lay. 'Now as the number of females in this island much exceeds that of the males; and, as, from the mild temperature of the climate circumstances frequently arise among the lower ranks that render the intention of this act of no effect; we could not help thinking this public exhibition of the abstract as rather a rigorous exertion of Justice.'

Another clerical champion of local beauties is the Rev. Warner in his account of a trip to Cornwall. 'The broad and muscular outline of the male, and the luxuriant *contour* of the female form, here, evince that the climate, food or employment of the people (or perhaps all together)

are highly conducive to the maturation and perfection
of the human figure.' He waxed lyrical over the softness
and roundness of the women and over their smooth skin,
reaching the unlikely conclusion that all was a result of
their sticking to a diet of salted pilchards. Sadly, this
testament to Cornish beauty was not corroborated by
another visitor, the potter Josiah Wedgwood, who
recorded in his diary a meeting with two women's sick
clubs in Truro. 'I am sorry I cannot say much in favour
of the beauty of this groupe of the fair sex, indeed there
were scarcely three faces in the two clubs that were
tolerable.'

The last candidates for the beauty contest were brought
forward by W. Hutchinson who was distracted from the
usual tourist pleasures of viewing picturesque lakes and
mountains by the sight of Lakeland women. 'The women
of this country are remarkably beautiful – the bold un-
intelligent stare, the fluttering inconsistent pertness and
lisping nonsense, so characteristic of the sex in southern
counties are here totally neglected for intelligent looks
cloathed in modesty, and politeness united with simplicity
of manners.'

So each region had its champions but the last word
ought perhaps to be reserved for the one tourist who
achieved the remarkable distinction of commenting on
the work of a group of women without mentioning their
looks at all. E. D. Clarke wrote in Plymouth: 'It is usual
in this part of the world, to see women employed in the
management of the ferry-boats. We were conducted, on
our return from the dock, by two of these nautical females.
From the skill which they evinced in feathering the oars,
and their dexterity in managing the sails, I do not see why
His Majesty's navy might not be supplied upon emer-
gencies, with these aquatic amazons.'

It was left to the foreign visitors such as Prince Pückler-
Muskau to note oddities among the English natives.
'If colds and consumptions are frequent in England, it
is more to be attributed to the people than to the climate.
They have a peculiar predilection for walks on the wet

grass; and in every public room there are open windows, so that it is hardly possible to bear the drafts. Even when they are shut the wind whistles through them; for they are seldom substantial and never double.'

Looking back through the eighteenth-century travellers' accounts of the way of life of ordinary people, certain features stand out. First, there is the extreme curiosity with which they viewed the oddities of their fellow men. The victims of this scrutiny may not always have welcomed it but now and again they found something to stare at themselves. Wigstead found Dolgellau to be almost in a state of insurrection, and all because a tourist had arrived with a black servant. The locals thought they had seen the devil or worse. All in all, however, the Georgian tourists' curiosity is preferable to the dulled senses of his latter day equivalent whose only contact with the local population comes when he orders food from a waiter. The second point one notices is that regional differences were much more marked than they are today – and often in quite different ways. North Wales, for example, is now associated in many minds with Methodism and pubs that close on Sundays – certainly not with bundling, nude bathing parties and boozy funerals. But perhaps the strongest impression is of tradition being given a new meaning. We are so used to seeing 'traditional' costumes and 'traditional' customs being trotted out for special occasions that we tend to forget that they were once simply a part of the everyday life of the British: blind harpists did play to travellers, Welsh women really did wear tall hats. The accounts help to give back to tradition a basis in reality.

7

End of an Age

═══

THE first age of tourism came to an end, if one wants
to put an exact date to it, on 15 September 1830. On that
date was opened the Liverpool and Manchester railway.
It was not, of course, the first railway. That honour
goes to the Stockton and Darlington railway opened
in 1825, but that was intended principally for freight,
and passengers who travelled it were carried in horse-
drawn trains. So to the Liverpool and Manchester went
the laurels of beginning the first regular passenger
service on the new steam railways. What an event
the opening was! It was estimated that some 40,000
spectators lined the route, swarming over buildings and
banks, perching on steep cutting sides and bridges.
The Duke of Wellington was there in a splendid carriage,
painted in scarlet and gold, and no fewer than eight
locomotives pulling eight trains took part in the triumphant progress. The greatest excitement of all was felt
by those lucky enough to have a seat on the train for
this occasion. Here is the Rev. Edward Stanley describing the experience for the readers of *Blackwood's
Magazine*.

No words can convey an adequate notion of the
magnificence (I cannot use a smaller word) of our
progress. At first it was comparatively slow; but
soon we felt we were indeed GOING, and then it
was that every person to whom the conveyance was
new, must have been sensible that the adaptation
of locomotive power was establishing a fresh era

in the state of society: the final results of which it was impossible to contemplate.

A new era indeed, and one consequence was a decisive change in the pattern of tourism. As the railways spread, so the 'foreign' parts of Britain seemed to be pulled closer together. Transport was not only to become quicker but also cheaper, and both factors were to change the nature of tourism. In 1840 nearly two and a half thousand passengers were carried on a single excursion train, and at least one young man, Thomas Cook, was sufficiently impressed to decide to devote his life to building up the tourist trade on the railways. It was a somewhat modest affair, carrying passengers in open trucks from Leicester to Loughborough, but it was a beginning. Speed was the key to it all. Speed meant that a trip to the 'remote' Lake District, instead of requiring careful planning and a minimum of two weeks' touring, could be made in a fraction of the time, until at last the day excursion came to play a dominant part in the tourist business. Lower costs meant that far more people could travel and those who could never have dreamed of taking a two weeks' holiday, let alone a two month tour, could manage a day trip or even a weekend jaunt. But the short trip meant a different attitude on the part of the tourist. The Georgian travellers had time and leisure in plenty to explore, to enquire, to go and find things out for themselves. The new generation had no time for such luxuries. If you have only one weekend to see the Lake District, then you want to see the famous beauty spots, not the paupers. And if you have come as an escape from the new industrial centres, then you are certainly not going to spend that precious spare time looking at carpet factories. The changing tempo of travel led inevitably to changing attitudes.

To meet the needs of the new tourists, new travel books were prepared, of which the most curious – and yet most appropriate to the changing times – was Edward Churton's *Rail Road Book of England*. It begins with a

description of intent which could have fitted easily enough
into the earlier guides. The author set out to describe 'the
cities, towns, country-seats, and picturesque scenery'
through which the railway traveller might pass. There
the similarities end. The old-time traveller could stop
his carriage or post-chaise to see just what he wanted
to – even the stage-coach passengers had regular halts
where they could get out and inspect the scenery. Not
so the new generation of railway passenger speeding
through the country. What he needed was a new type of
guide, one that would tell him just what it was that he
was being whisked past at such a rate. Mr Churton's
guide is conveniently arranged – on the left hand page
there is information about what the passenger may see
by glancing out of the left hand carriage window, while
the right hand page gives details of the view on the other
side. Very helpful, unless of course one happened to be
travelling in the opposite direction, when it might prove
a little confusing. As even railway passengers had to
stop somewhere, the guide also gave information on
each and every town and village through which the
tracks passed. Some of this was relevant and useful,
some rather less so. While there was a clear advantage
in knowing that Romford's market days were Tuesday
and Wednesday, it is more difficult to think what use
the traveller might have made of the information that
the parish covered 3,340 acres. What is very obvious,
however, is that travel books had entered a new age.
So too had travellers: the post-chaise traveller became
the steam railway traveller; Georgian Britain became
Victorian Britain. A new age of tourism was to follow.

The first age of British tourism lasted for little more
than half a century, and the first British tourists came
from a distinctly narrow social stratum. Yet they have
left us a unique legacy, a colourful picture of their time.
They viewed the country at a critical moment of change
and captured that moment for us. Most important of
all the traits of the Georgian tourists was the one we
have come back to time and time again – that pervasive

curiosity, that led them to poke into every corner of life. There were few places that the travellers visited where they failed to find something new and exciting to record. It was all perfectly expressed by one of the first and perhaps the greatest of all the early travel writers, Daniel Defoe, in words that could stand as a motto for all those travellers who came after him.

Where-ever we come, and which way soever we look, we see something new, something significant, something well worth the traveller's stay, and the writer's care; nor is any check to our design, or obstruction to its acceptance in the world, to say the like has been done already, or to panegyrick upon the labours and value of those authors who have gone before, in this work: A compleat account of Great Britain will be the work of many years, I might say ages, and may employ many hands. Whoever has travell'd Great Britain before us, and whatever they have written, tho' they may have had a harvest, yet they have always, either by necessity, ignorance or negligence pass'd over so much, that others may come and glean after them by large handfuls.

Bibliography

This list contains details of all the works quoted in the main text. It does not include those which were consulted but not quoted and it is not intended as a complete guide to tourist accounts of the period.

'Account of the Stage Coaches and Carriers', *The London Directory*, 1776

Aikin, Arthur, *Journal of a Tour through North Wales*, 1797

Beaumont, George and Disney, Captain Henry, *A New Tour through England, performed in the summers of 1765, 1766, & 1767*, 1768

Boswell, James, *A Journal of a Tour to the Hebrides with Samuel Johnson LLD*, 1786

Bray, William, *Sketch of a Tour into Derbyshire and Yorkshire*, 1783

Byng, John, Viscount Torrington, *Diaries*, 1792 (published 1936)

Clarke, E. D., *Tour Through the South of England, Wales and Part of Ireland, 1791*, 1793

Combe, Richard, *The Tour of Doctor Syntax*, 1812

Coxe, William, *Historical Tour through Monmouthshire*, 1801

Cradock, J., *Letters from Snowdon*, 1770

Defoe, Daniel, *A Tour through the Whole Island of Great Britain*, 1724–6

Evans, Rev. J., *A Tour through Part of North Wales in the year 1797, and at other times*, 1798

Fielding, T. H., *Scenery of the Lakes*, 1822

Gilpin, William, *Observations on the Mountains and Lakes of Cumberland and Westmoreland*, 1786

—— *Observations on the River Wye*, 1770

—— *On Landscape Painting, A Poem in Picturesque Subjects*, 1808

Bibliography

Grant, J., *Journal of a Three Weeks Tour in 1797 through Derbyshire to the Lakes*, 1798

Hanway, Mary Ann, *A Journey to the Highlands of Scotland*, 1777

Hassell, J., *Tour of the Isle of Wight*, 1790

Heron, Robert, *Observations made in a Journey through the Western Counties of Scotland in 1792*, 1799

Hurtley, Thomas, *Natural Curiosities of Malham*, 1786

Hutchinson, W., *An Excursion to the Lakes*, 1776

Hutton, William, *The Scarborough Tour in 1803*, 1804

Johnson, Samuel, *A Journey to the Western Islands of Scotland*, 1775

Kitchiner, Doctor William, *The Traveller's Oracle*, 1827

Lipscomb, George, *Journey into South Wales in the Year 1799*, 1802

MacRitchie, William, *Diary of a Tour through Great Britain in 1795*, 1897

Maton, William George, *Observations Relative Chiefly to the Natural History, Picturesque Scenery and Antiquities of the Western Counties of England, 1794 & 6*, 1797

Mavor, William, *The British Tourist*, 1809

—— *Tour in Wales and through Several Counties of England in 1805*, 1806

Morgan, Mary, *A Tour to Milford Haven in the Year 1791*, 1795

Moritz, Charles, *Travels in England*, 1782

Pennant, Thomas, *Journey from Chester to London*, 1782

—— *Tour from Alston Moor to Harrowgate & Brimham Crags 1773*, 1804

—— *Tour in Scotland*, 1771

—— *A Tour in Wales*, 1784

Pichot, A., *Tour of a Foreigner in England and Scotland*, 1825

Pückler-Muskau, Prince, *Tour in England, Ireland & France in the Years 1828, 1829, 1832*

Rutland, Duke of, *Journal of a Tour Through North and South Wales*, 1805

—— *Journal of a Tour in the Northern Parts of Great Britain*, 1796

St-Fond, Bartholemew Faujas de, *Travels in England, Scotland and the Hebrides*, 1799

Shaw, Stebbing, *A Tour of the West of England in 1788*, 1789

Skrine, Henry, *Three Successive Tours in the North of England and Great Part of Scotland*, 1795

Skrine, Henry, *Two Successive Tours Throughout the Whole of Wales*, 1798

Southey, Robert, *Journal of a Tour in Scotland in 1819*, 1929

Warner, Rev. Richard, *Excursions from Bath*, 1801

—— *A Second Walk through Wales in August and September 1798*, 1799

—— *A Tour Through Cornwall in the Autumn of 1808*, 1809

—— *A Tour Through the Northern Counties of England and the Borders of Scotland*, 1802

—— *A Walk through some of the Western Counties of England*, 1800

Webb, Daniel Carless, *Observations and Remarks During Four Excursions made to various parts of Great Britain 1810, 1811, 1812*

West, Mr, *A Guide to the Lakes in Cumberland, Westmoreland and Lancashire*, 1784

Wigstead, Henry, *Remarks on a Tour to North and South Wales in 1797*, 1800

Wyndham, Henry Penruddocke, *A Tour through Wales*, 1781

—— *A Picture of the Isle of Wight delineated upon the spot in the year 1793*, 1794

Young, Arthur, *A Six Months Tour through the North of England*, 1769

Index

===

Aberystwyth, 26, 72, 133
Aiken, Arthur, 90, 114, 132
Alexander, Mrs, 102
Alnwick castle, 50–1, 56–7
Amlwch, 114–15
Arkwright, Sir Richard, 57, 91–2, 107
Austen, Jane, 40, 69–70
Aysgarth, 91

Bala, 47
Bangor, 72–3
Banks, Sir Joseph, 15, 62
Barnard's Castle, 117–18
Barrington, Mr, 135
Barton aqueduct, 76–7
Basingstoke, 21
Bath, 67–9
Beaumont, George, 29
Bideford, 99
Birmingham, 94–6, 108, 119
Blaenavon, 83
Blenheim, 54, 59, 60
Boswell, James, 122, 123–4
Boulton and Watt, 95–6, 97
Bournemouth, 71
Bray, William, 92, 109
Brecknock, 128
Brecon, 41
Brecon and Abergavenny Canal, 81–2
Bridgewater Canal, 26, 76–7, 80–1, 85
Brindley, James, 77, 101
Brown, Dr John, 37–8
Buckinghamshire lace makers, 107–108
Burslem, 97, 98, 99
Butler, Lady Eleanor, 129–30
Byng, John, Viscount Torrington
    at Cromford, 57
    collecting brasses, 62
    and cotton mills, 91–2
    on industrial workers, 108–9

Caerphilly, 26–7
Caerwent, 62–3
Caerwys, 133, 134
Caledonian Canal, 79–80
Cambridge, 67
Capel Curig, 46
Cardigan, 26
Carroll, Lewis, 32
Carron iron works, 84, 85
Castle Howard, 26
Chatsworth, 57, 58
Chester, 16, 62
Chippenham, 19
Churton, Edward, 142–3
Clarke, E. D., 26, 45
    on picturesque, 40
    at Ryddol Falls, 47
    at Shakespeare's birthplace, 65
    on Oxford, 67
    at Bath, 68–9
    at Swansea, 83
    visits mines, 86–7
    visits Wedgwood, 100
    on Welsh, 128, 133, 136
    on boatwomen, 139
Claude Lorrain, 33, 38
Coalbrookdale, 84
Combe, Richard, 31
Coniston, 39–40
Cook, Thomas, 142
Cornwall, people and customs, 138–139
Coxe, William, 83
Cradock, J., 44
Craven lead mines, 109
Cromford, 57, 91–2

Dale, David, 112–13
Darby iron works, 84
Darnly, Henry, 63
Defoe, Daniel, 32, 33, 67–8, 72, 144
Devil's Arse Cavern, 15
Devil's Bridge, 46
Disney, Captain Henry, 29

149

Doncaster, 60
Dovedale, 67, 68
Dowlais iron works, 82–3, 84

Eaglehurst, 58
Edinburgh, 19, 127
Eisteddfod, 133, 134
England,
  people and customs, 137–40
Etruria, 96–7
Evans, Rev. J., 129–30

Fielding, T. H., 49
Fingal's Cave, 48–9
Fort William, 79
Fountains Abbey, 50

Gilpin, William, 49, 60
  principles of picturesque, 33–5,
    39
  and Wye Valley, 35–7
Glasgow, 127
Gloucester, 15
Goodrich castle, 35
Gordale Scar, 42–3
Grant, J., 110–11
Gretna Green, 122–3
Guilford, Lord, 57
Gwyneddigion Society, 134

Hanway, Mary Ann, 56–7, 125–6,
  127
Harecastle tunnel, 78–9
Harrison, John, 101
Harrogate, 69
Hassell, J., 58, 63–4, 138
Herculaneum, 61
Heron, Robert, 115
Holyrood, 63
Hurtley, Thomas, 30, 42–3
Hutchinson, W., 27, 112, 117–18,
  139
Hutton, William
  on stage coach travel, 21
  at York, 60–1
  at Scarborough, 70–1
  at Sheffield, 104
  on debtors, 111

Inns, 17, 26–8, 105
Inverary Castle, 104–5
Iona, 124–5

Johnson, Dr Samuel, 32–3, 122,
  123–4

Kendal, 32
Keswick, 37–8

Kitchiner, Dr William, 17, 18, 19,
  20–1, 24–6
Kiverton, 55

Lake District, 31, 37–40, 49, 105
  women of, 139
Leadhills, 115
Lipscomb, George, 119
Liverpool and Manchester Railway,
  141–2
Llangollen, 78
  Ladies of, 129–30
Llanrhaids, 47
Longleat, 59, 60
Lyme Regis, 69–70

MacRitchie, Rev. William, 94, 138
Malvern Hills, 43–4
Manchester, 17, 26, 93–4, 108, 117
Matlock, 69, 93
Maton, W. G., 131
Mavor, William
  life, 12–13
  on Powis Castle, 55–6
  on Oxford and Cambridge, 67
  sea-bathing in Wales, 73
  on Pontcysyllte, 78
  visits Worcester, 100
  on Welsh, 128, 131–2
  on bundling, 130–1
Merthyr Tydfil, 41, 82–3
Milford Haven, 41–2
Morgan, Mary
  on women writers, 29–30
  at seaside, 41–2
  at Blenheim, 59
  on lace makers, 107–8
  visits miners, 116
  on Welsh, 128–9, 131, 132, 133,
    134, 137
Moritz, Charles, 19–20, 22, 66
Muxmore, 92–3

Nash, Beau, 68
Newcastle-under-Lime, 97, 98
Newcastle-upon-Tyne, 85
New Lanark, 112–14
Newport, Isle of Wight, 138
Norfolk, Duke of, 104
Northampton, 109
Northwich, 87

Owen, Robert, 113
Oxford, 15, 54, 66–7

Parys Mountain, 89–90, 114
Peak District, 33, 69, 92

Pennant, Thomas, 22
  life, 13–14
  on Chester gaol, 15–16
  on Snowdon, 44–5
  at Fountains Abbey, 50
  on Alnwick Castle, 56
  at Holyrood, 63
  at Brimham Crags, 64
  at Parys Mountain, 90
  on Scots, 105–6, 125, 126–7
  on workhouse, 112
  at Leadhills, 115–16
  on Eisteddfod, 133
Penrith, 27, 112
Pichot, A., 30–1, 110
Plymouth, 139
Poldeis mine, 86–7
Pompeii, 61
Ponsonby, Sarah, 129–30
Pontcysyllte, 78
Portland, 131
Poussin, Gaspard, 33, 38
Powis Castle, 55–6
Priestley, Joseph, 101
Pückler-Muskau, Prince
  on British hospitality, 27–9
  on Welsh mountains, 46
  at Warwick Castle, 51–3
  at Woburn, 58–9
  at Harrogate, 69
  sea bathing, 72–3
  at Tintern iron works, 84
  visits slate quarry, 88–9
  at Birmingham, 94
  on the poor, 105–6
  on Welsh funerals, 136
  on English, 139–40

Radcliffe, Mrs, 45
Reynolds, Joshua, 55
Rockingham, Marquis of, 55
Romford, 143
Rotherham, 26, 97
Rubens, Peter Paul, 55, 56
Rutland, Duke of
  sailing, 23–4
  in South Wales, 41, 81–2
  at St Andrew's, 50
  at Whitby, 70–1
  at New Lanark, 112–13
  at Methodist service, 119
Ryddol Falls, 46, 47

St Andrew's, 50
St-Fond, Bartholomew Faujas de
  visits anatomist, 14–15
  on inns, 17
  at Fingal's cave, 48–9

  on Tyneside, 75–6
  at Carron iron works, 85
  visits James Watt, 95–6
  meals in Scotland, 102–4
  at Inverary Castle, 104–5
  and Scots hospitality, 124–5
  on Scots women, 127–8
Scarborough, 54, 70–1
Scotland,
  people and customs, 122–8
Shakespeare, William, 64–6
Shaw, Rev. Stebbing
  visiting prisons, 15, 16
  on Malverns, 43–4
  at Oxford, 66
  in Harecastle tunnel, 78–9
  visits cloth mill, 92–3
Sheffield, 96–7, 104, 108, 117
Sheldon, John, 14–15
Shepherd, Mr, 21–2
Sidney, Sir Philip, 30
Skiddaw, 45
Skrine, Henry
  at Alnwick Castle, 50–1
  in York Minster, 60
  at Stratford-upon-Avon, 64
  at Worsley, 77
  at Coalbrookdale, 84
  in Potteries, 97–8
  in Scotland, 122–3
Snowdon, 44–5
  slate quarry, 88–9
South Kyne, 62
Southey, Robert, 79–80, 113–14
Staffa, 48–9, 124
Stanley, Rev. Edward, 141
Stockton and Darlington Railway,
  141
Stonehenge, 63–4
Stratford-upon-Avon, 54, 64–6
Stroud, 92, 93
Stukely, William, 61–2
Sullivan, R. J., 85
Swansea, 112
Swinton, 109

Telford, Thomas, 79
Tenby, 23–4
Thornton, William, 48, 124
Tintern Abbey, 35–7
Tintern iron works, 83–4
Titian, 55
Travel,
  on horseback, 14
  costs of, 17
  by stage coach, 18–21
  by post chaise, 21
  on foot, 21–3

Index

Travel–*cont.*
  by boat, 23–4, 80–1
  equipment for, 24–6
Trecastle, 128–9
Trent and Mersey Canal, 78–9
Truro, 86, 139
Tryfan, 46
Tucker, Samuel, 97
Tyneside, 75–6

Vanbrugh, Sir John, 60

Wales,
  people and customs, 72–3, 119–
    121, 128–37
Wanlockhead, 115
Warner, Rev. Richard, 15, 22–3
  at Longleat, 59
  on Vanbrugh, 60
  visits Boulton and Watt, 94–5
  in Potteries, 97
  supper in Wales, 105
  on lead miners, 109
  on bundling, 131
  on Welsh, 134, 135–6, 136–7
  on Cornish, 138–9
Warwick Castle, 51–3
Watt, James, 95–6, 101
Wedgwood, Josiah, 97–100, 139
Wedgwood, Josiah II, 62–3
Wedgwood, Sukey, 72
Wellington, Duke of, 141
Wentworth House, 54–5

West, Mr, 39–40
Whitby, 70–1
Whitehaven, 112
Wigan, 23
Wight, Isle of, 138
Wigstead, Henry, 94–5, 137
Woburn, 54, 57, 58–9
Woodstock, 12
  see also, Blenheim
Worcester, 100
Wordsworth, William, 39
Worsley, 77
Wroxton, 57
Wyndham, Henry Penruddocke
  at Caerphilly, 26–7
  on Welsh guides, 47
  on Welsh poor, 119–21
  on Welsh customs, 135, 136, 137
Wye valley, 33, 34–7, 84

York, 54, 60–1, 111
Young, Arthur, 15
  on roads, 23
  on inns, 26
  on stately homes, 54–5
  at Alnwick Castle, 56
  at Doncaster, 60
  on York Minster, 60
  at Sheffield, 96–7
  on Potteries, 98–9
  on industrial work, 101, 117
  on miners, 109